pat y

explo od

by members of the Faith and Order Advisory Group

edited by Paul Avis

CHURCH HOUSE
PUBLISHING

Church House Publishing
Church House
Great Smith Street
London SW1P 3NZ

Tel: 020 7898 1451
Fax: 020 7898 1449

ISBN 0 7151 5768 X

GS Misc 742

Published 2004 for the Council for
Christian Unity of the Archbishops'
Council by Church House Publishing

Typeset in Franklin Gothic 9.5/11pt

Printed in England by
The Cromwell Press Ltd,
Trowbridge, Wiltshire

The Faith and Order Advisory Group
advises the Council for Christian
Unity and the House of Bishops
on ecumenical and ecclesiological
questions. The chapters of this
book are the result of a process
of study and discussion within
FOAG but the contributors are
responsible for the views expressed
in their own essays.

contents

Contributors

The Revd Prebendary Dr Paul Avis — General Secretary of the Council for Christian Unity; Sub-Dean of Exeter

Dr Martin Davie — Theological Secretary of the Council for Christian Unity and Theological Consultant to the House of Bishops

The Revd Canon Peter Fisher — Vicar of St Peter, Maney, Birmingham; formerly Principal of The Queen's Foundation, Birmingham

Dr Paula Gooder — Lecturer at The Queen's College, Birmingham; formerly Tutor at Ripon College Cuddesdon

The Rt Revd Christopher Hill — Bishop of Stafford, Vice-Chairman of FOAG

The Revd Canon Dr Joy Tetley — Archdeacon of Worcester

The Revd Professor John Webster — Professor of Systematic Theology in the University of Aberdeen; formerly Lady Margaret Professor of Divinity in the University of Oxford and Canon of Christ Church

foreword

The background to this collection of essays lies in the current situation of the ecumenical movement. As Paul Avis puts it, 'The ecumenical movement seems to have reached a watershed. Its momentum slowed noticeably in the last decade of the twentieth century. In the first decade of the new century it is definitely faltering.'[1] However we evaluate the present state of the Christian quest for the full visible unity of Christ's disciples, it is clear that some interpretation is needed as ecumenism enters a new stage.

The reasons for the present malaise are varied. The enthusiasm and high hopes of the years following the Second Vatican Council were followed by some disappointments as apparently promising ventures came to nothing and suggested timetables proved unrealistically optimistic. At the same time, it became increasingly clear that both the doctrinal differences between Churches and the connection between doctrinal accords and changed ecclesial relationships are more complex than sometimes appear. A further factor was the entry into ecumenical dialogue of church traditions not previously involved. Moreover, especially in Churches with a relatively broad or comprehensive membership, voices have recently been raised indicating that not everyone feels in sympathy with the official approaches taken by their Church to questions of Christian unity.

At a time like this, a degree of uncertainty is therefore understandable for those who have been committed to the kind of ecumenism represented by the Faith and Order Commission of the World Council of Churches and the major bilateral dialogues between the world communions. The Church of England, in particular, has directed its ecumenical endeavours towards the full visible unity of the Church, 'all round and at every level', and to be sought by stages. Such an approach has fitted in well with the celebrated Chicago–Lambeth Quadrilateral and is illustrated by relations with the Roman Catholic Church (primarily at the global level through the work of the Anglican–Roman Catholic International Commission (ARCIC) and the International Anglican–Roman Catholic Commission for Unity and Mission (IARCCUM)). It is also illustrated by Anglican–Lutheran relations, although in this case it must be admitted that significant differences are to be seen between the practical outworking of the dialogue in different parts of the world.

Taken together, such issues define the present moment as one in which the ecumenical movement as a whole needs to become more self-reflective. As well as the obvious need to address the doctrinal and the so-called non-theological factors dividing the Churches, it is necessary to consider the methods by which they are to be addressed and to map out the methodological processes which either do or should underlie the quest for church unity. Indeed, even the idea of unity itself is far from simple and discussion of ecumenical method cannot avoid questions about the goal of ecumenism and the nature of unity.

Such considerations do not occur in a vacuum, however. The very word 'ecumenism' gives the game away. Its ancestry is as much political as theological and immediately raises questions about the place of church unity (and of what kind?) as a reflection or a servant of human community (imperial, national unity or global.) The idea of a single inhabited world (*oikoumene*), and the need for a common ideology for it, is very ancient.

Christians in every generation need, however, to ask what kind of unity in their own day arises from the apostles' witness. In doing so they have to revisit the original causes for division and assess the issues that perpetuate division today. This in turn opens the possibility for re-evaluating disagreements and misunderstandings, and for considering the extent to which they require or justify continued separation.

Most Churches are now able to recognize a distinction between the faith and its formulations in such a way as to enable those involved in ecumenical dialogue to look together at controversial issues. In an earlier report the Faith and Order Advisory Group of the Church of England, which has also sponsored the present collection of essays, expressed the matter like this:

> While not denying that serious issues have divided the churches, commitment to the possibility of convergence entails acknowledging that emotive and polarized language has played a large part in continuing the separation of the churches. The process of convergence involves a willingness to leave behind the language of past polemic in the search for a common understanding. All the dialogues look for ways of reconciling antithetical positions, avoiding the terms in which the antithesis was originally put forward. This method suggests that whatever may have been the case in the past is now no longer necessarily so. While there can be no justification in theological dialogue for glossing over differences, it is accepted that the pursuit of

restatement is possible. That is, not more eirenic statements of where we once were, nor even restatements of where we are now in our separation, but restatements of our common Christian heritage. The dialogues, therefore, avoid controversial language and attempt to re-examine and re-appropriate our common heritage offered to us in the scriptures and Tradition.[2]

A recent exciting example of the possibilities of this approach was the Joint Declaration on Justification signed in 1999 by the Lutheran World Federation and the Roman Catholic Church. In evaluating together one of the areas of doctrine which have proved so divisive in the past, these two Communions have been able to recognize that in their actual teaching today 'a consensus in basic truths of the doctrine of justification exists between Lutherans and Catholics'. It follows that 'the doctrinal condemnations of the sixteenth century, in so far as they relate to the doctrine of justification, appear in a new light' and those mutual condemnations do not apply to the teachings of the signatory Churches today.

This collection of essays is offered as a contribution to the debate about ecumenical method, in which much is too often taken for granted and in which implicitly held assumptions about one's own approaches and those of others can seriously hinder mutual understanding. The authors are all members of the Faith and Order Advisory Group of the Church of England and have worked together both in the group itself and in a working party on the question of method in ecumenical dialogue for a number of years. While they have therefore benefited from each other's insights and from the wider work of FOAG on matters of ecumenical or theological concern, the book does not therefore set out to be a definitive statement of Anglican ecumenical method. This may clearly be seen by the questions addressed to some aspects of the official Church of England approach to the quest for the unity of the Church. Moreover, as befits a series of explorations in ecumenical method, no attempt has been made to harmonize the contributions or arrive at an agreed statement. All agree, however, about the seriousness of the issues at stake, the need for clarity of understanding and expression, and, very centrally, on the importance of sound hermeneutic principles in the handling of biblical material in ecumenical dialogue.

There are, of course, limitations to any such collection, coming as it does out of a particular context. The ecumenical movement is, for example, beginning to have to take account of similar questions arising in the context of interfaith dialogue. Even within the strict limits of Christian ecumenism, it is not easy to find a language which does justice both to the concerns of the 'Western' Churches and to those of the 'global South' whose voices are becoming increasingly urgent.

On 11 September 2001 FOAG was in the middle of its annual residential meeting. Nothing could have more focused the minds of members of the group on the wider world context of the ecumenical quest than the image of the twin towers. It is our hope in this volume to make a modest but serious contribution to Christian reflection on why unity matters and what kind of unity best serves God's purposes for a divided world.

✠ John Cicester
Chairman, Faith and Order Advisory Group

chapter one

the goals of ecumenism

John Webster

'full, visible unity'

Over the course of the last couple of decades, mainstream Anglican
ecumenists have stated the goal of the reconciliation of the
Churches with increasing precision as that of full, visible unity.[1]
This can readily be demonstrated by a reading of a good number
of primary ecumenical documents from the international dialogues
in which Anglicans have been partners and from the conversations
in which the Church of England has been engaged. As a result of
ecumenical theological work and of ecumenical fellowship, the wider
Anglican and the Church of England's ecumenical strategy have
been directed fairly consistently towards that goal, and full, visible
unity has become the standard description of the goal which thirty-
eight years ago Pope Paul VI and Archbishop Ramsey called
perfecta communio fidei et vitae sacramentalis in their 1966
Common Declaration.[2]

In this respect, Anglican self-understanding reflects developments
in the wider ecumenical climate, particularly in the World Council of
Churches, which have both set much of the pace for denominational
conversations and, of course, drawn upon their resources. There is
no space here for a full review of the materials, but the story can be
picked up from the 1961 New Delhi Assembly, whose report states:

> We believe that the unity which is both God's call and his gift to
> his Church is made visible as all in each place who are baptized
> into Jesus Christ and confess him as Lord and Saviour are
> brought by the Holy Spirit into one fully committed fellowship,
> holding the one apostolic faith, preaching the one Gospel,
> breaking the one bread, joining in common prayer, and having
> a corporate life reaching out in witness and service to all, and
> who at the same time are united with the whole Christian
> fellowship in all places and ages in such ways that ministry
> and members are accepted by all, and that all can act and
> speak together as occasion requires for the tasks to which God
> calls his people.[3]

Already the rudiments of what will later be articulated as full, visible unity are there. Unity is to be visible, that is, it must have some kind of public, historical form, and the form of the visibility is sacramental unity, common confession and witness, and (in some shape) a ministry acceptable to all through which common mission can be pursued. By 1975 at Nairobi, the conception had been (depending on your point of view) either somewhat refined or somewhat muddled, largely through development of the notion of 'conciliar fellowship' which had emerged earlier at the 1968 Uppsala Assembly. Thus Nairobi suggested that

> The one Church is to be envisioned as a conciliar fellowship of local churches which are themselves truly united. In this conciliar fellowship each local church possesses, in communion with the others, the fullness of catholicity, witnesses to the same apostolic faith and therefore recognises the others as belonging to the same Church of Christ and guided by the same Spirit.

Moreover, Nairobi continues,

> They are bound together because they have the same baptism, and share in the same eucharist; they recognise each other's members and ministries. They are one in their common commitment to confess the Gospel of Christ by proclamation and service to the world. To this end, each church aims at maintaining sustained and sustaining relationships with her sister churches, expressed in conciliar gatherings whenever required for the fulfilment of their common calling.[4]

As is well known, the notion of conciliar fellowship evoked different interpretations: some read it as roughly equivalent to visible unity; others as something rather less, perhaps as a federal model. Both the 1982 Vancouver Assembly and that in Canberra ten years later attempted to clarify matters by identifying three marks of a united Church: a common confession of the apostolic faith; a mutual recognition of baptism, Eucharist and ministry which constitutes what Vancouver called 'visible communion' and Canberra called 'full communion'; and common instruments of consultation and decision-making to serve the mission of the Church (this latter received slightly less emphasis at Canberra, however).

Something of the same kind of development – a concentration upon the visibility of unity, and an attempt to spell out the identifying marks of such visibility – can be seen in Anglican documents from around the same period. Thus, for example, ARCIC I proposes that 'Unity is of the essence of the Church, and since the Church is visible its unity must also be visible';[5] slightly more sharply, ARCIC II states that 'The purpose of our dialogue is the restoration of full ecclesial communion between us.'[6]

The same theme surfaces in Anglican–Lutheran discussions. The Niagara Report, for example, notes that 'Because of all that we share, we concur with the conclusion of the Anglican–Lutheran European Regional Commission: "There are no longer any serious obstacles on the way towards the establishment of full communion between our two Churches".'[7] More recently, however, these various conceptions (visible unity, full communion, full ecclesial communion) have stabilized into the notion of full, visible unity. The clearest articulation of this can be found in the Meissen Agreement, which is worth citing at some length:

> [I]n a fallen world we are committed to strive for the 'full, visible unity' of the body of Christ on earth ... As the Churches grow together the understanding of the characteristics of full, visible unity become clearer. We can already claim that full, visible unity must include:
>
> – a common confession of the apostolic faith in word and life ...
>
> – the sharing of one baptism, the celebrating of one eucharist and the service of reconciled, common ministry. This common participation in one baptism, one eucharist and one ministry unites 'all in each place' with 'all in every place' within the whole communion of saints ...
>
> – bonds of communion which enable the Church at every level to guard and interpret the apostolic faith, to take decisions, to teach authoritatively, to share goods and to bear effective witness in the world. The bonds of communion will possess personal, collegial and communal aspects ...[8]

The clarity and maturity of the Meissen Agreement has clearly commended itself widely: it is reproduced substantially in both the Reuilly Common Statement and the Fetter Lane Common Statement. Like the WCC documents to which reference has already been made, it emphasizes three marks of the unity of the Church (common confession; common sacraments and ministry; and some sort of common instruments of decision-making for the promotion of mission). But what is distinctive about Meissen and its derivatives is that it gives a rather more substantial account of the last of those three features. This is described as 'bonds of communion' which 'possess personal, collegial and communal aspects'. The expansion here is important for a couple of reasons. First, it bears out the fact that over the last two decades Anglicans have felt pressed to give a more detailed portraiture of their conception of the unity of the Church. Second, and more importantly, it tends to reinforce the conviction that episcopacy has to be a feature of any united Church. The phrase 'bonds of communion' may not suggest this immediately, but it is hard not to relate it to questions concerning episcopacy. Thus, for example, the Fetter Lane Common Statement, after quoting the Meissen material on 'bonds of communion', refers the reader on to a later paragraph in the Common Statement which glosses the phrase by saying

> A ministry of oversight (*episcope*) is a gift of God to the Church. In both our Churches it is exercised in personal, collegial and communal ways. It is necessary in order to witness to and safeguard the unity and apostolicity of the Church (Fetter Lane Common Statement, paragraph 28(j)).

This is, of course, in continuity with the kind of portrait of unity in ARCIC II (paragraph 45); though the notion of 'bonds of communion' is not utilized, it is clear that what ARCIC says about both a ministry of oversight and the episcopal ministry of a universal primate plays the same role as that of 'bonds of communion' in Meissen. Alongside and in addition to common confession and testimony, and common sacraments and ministry, full visible unity requires a further 'bond' through which it can be maintained.

It is worth at this point identifying, in an initial way at least, three oddities about the notion of 'bonds of communion'. What is odd, first, is the slenderness of the pneumatological basis of what is said, at least on the surface of the text – is not the *Spirit* the *vinculum communionis*? The Trinitarian theology which Meissen and derivatives share with most recent ecumenical statements clearly assumes that pneumatology is central; but the relation of the Spirit's work to the nature and exercise of *episcope* remains under-explored. Second, there is the oddity of adding 'bonds of communion' to common confession, common sacraments and common ministry; the effect tends to be to introduce some separation between *episcope* and common ministry. And third, there is the oddity of the notion of 'bonds'. Is what is referred to the 'bonds' of the Church's communion, or in fact the executive instruments of the unity of the institution? The generalization of the notion of oversight – its expansion into communal, collegial and personal – is not very helpful here, and may be the source of some of the lack of precision at this point.

But setting such quibbles aside for the moment, the basic commitment is clear. The trajectory along which Anglican ecumenical work has been proceeding for the last couple of decades has as its goal the full, visible unity of all Christians in each particular place with all Christians in every place. This goal functions not only as the terminus of ecumenical reconciliation but also as a way of measuring ecumenical progress, so that the reconciliation of the churches proceeds through what Fetter Lane (paragraphs 24–7) calls 'steps to full, visible unity', with the Church, as Meissen puts it, 'on the way to visible unity'.

Before moving on to discuss these developments, it is important to pause and identify two further convictions which are closely related to the notion of full, visible unity and which have emerged in the ecumenical literature. The first is the inseparability of ecumenism and mission. Anglican ecumenical documents have shared the general conviction that there is a missionary aspect to the pursuit of the goal of full visible unity: the Church's witness is damaged by disunity, and so ensuring the health of the Church's testimony to the world is integral to the goal of ecumenical reconciliation. A number of statements will serve to reinforce the point:

> It is essential to approach the question of unity among Christians in this missionary and eschatological context . . . The unity of the Church is not simply an end in itself because the Church does not exist for itself but for the glory of God and as a sign, instrument and first-fruits of his purpose to reconcile all things in heaven and earth through Christ.[9]

> Part of the challenge to Christians is this: how can we bear true witness to the good news of a God who accepts us unless we can accept one another?[10]

> God's plan is the unification of all things in Christ; that, and nothing less, is the goal. Before that goal is realized the Church has the task of embodying in all that it is, says and does the promise that the goal is realizable.[11]

> The Church, the body of Christ, must always be seen in this perspective as instrumental to God's ultimate purpose. The Church exists for the glory of God and to serve, in obedience to the mission of Christ, the reconciliation of humankind and of all creation . . . We are to work for the manifestation of unity at every level, a unity which is grounded in the life of the Holy Trinity and is God's purpose for the whole of creation.[12]

A second consideration concerns the dogmatic foundations on which the notion of full, visible unity rests. This, in my judgement, is a really central matter for discussion: we will not be saved by ecumenical earnestness if we allow our thinking to become loose or disorderly at this point. Moreover, whilst it is certainly a matter for gratitude that some fundamental dogmatic issues have been addressed in the course of the development of the notion of full, visible unity as our ecumenical goal (notably in Trinitarian theology and ecclesiology), there is need for continued vigilance lest the discussion settle too quickly into habits of thought or conclusions which, when they become the basis for further thought and practice, may be sheltered from critical appraisal. This, of course, is why dogmatics is a central task in the life of the Church and therefore in its ecumenical work. It is the office of dogmatics to serve the holiness, unity and witness of the Church of Jesus Christ by inquiring into the adequacy of the Church's thought, speech and practice – including its ecumenical practice – when measured by the light of the gospel. In the context of ecumenism, dogmatics will have a particular interest in reflective inquiry into the conceptions of the Church which are presupposed, and, more deeply, into the understandings of the nature and purposes of God and of God's relation to the world which surface in an account of the goal of ecumenical reconciliation. This – emphatically – does not mean that dogmaticians are magistrates, summoning ecumenists before the bench and handing out cautions or sentences for doctrinal misconduct. Dogmatics is simply the Church attempting humbly, prayerfully, repentantly and under the tutelage of Holy Scripture, to envisage the truth so that it can act truthfully, that is, in accordance with the gospel.

A reading of the ecumenical literature suggests that the claim that the goal of ecumenism is full, visible unity is bound up with three interrelated dogmatic convictions: a certain understanding of the doctrine of the Trinity, and, more especially, of the nature of the relations both between the persons of the Trinity and between the triune God and the world; a certain understanding of the nature and purposes of the economy of salvation; and a certain understanding of the nature of the Church and of the place of the one Church in that saving economy. Set out in skeletal form, the basic claims go something like this:

1. a Trinitarian principle – the unity of the Church is grounded in the unity of the triune God, for God is confessed in the Christian tradition as the mutual and open fellowship of the divine persons, Father, Son and Spirit;

2. a soteriological principle – the economy of salvation is best understood as the history of the triune God's work of restoring humanity to fellowship with or participation in the inner divine fellowship;

3. an ecclesiological principle – the visible Church is the sign, foretaste or embodiment of the reconciliation of humanity with itself and with God.

Some representative quotations from ecumenical materials will show how these convictions operate:

[S]haring in the same Holy Spirit, whereby we become members of the same body of Christ and adopted children of the same Father, we are also bound to one another in a completely new relationship. *Koinonia* with one another is entailed by our *koinonia* with God in Christ. This is the mystery of the Church.[13]

God the Holy Trinity is one, a unity in diversity. He is the ground, source and pattern of all true unity . . . This vision of unity grounded in the very nature and being of the Triune God can leave us in no doubt that denominational divisions are both contrary to the will of God and, moreover, call into question the Church's mission in the world.[14]

The will of God, Father, Son and Holy Spirit, is to reconcile to himself all that he has created and sustains, to set free the creation from its bondage to decay, and to draw all humanity into communion with himself . . . Through baptism we are united with Christ in his death and resurrection, and by the power of the Spirit made members of one body, and together participate in the life of God.[15]

Today we are re-discovering . . . the communal character of the Church. Underlying many of the New Testament descriptions of the Church . . . is the reality of a *koinonia* – a communion – which is the sharing of the life of the Holy Trinity and therein with our fellow-members of the Church. This community – *koinonia* – according to the Scriptures is established by a baptism inseparable from faith and conversion. The vocation of all the baptised is to live as a corporate priesthood offering praise to God, sharing the good news and engaging in mission and service to humankind. This common life is sustained and nurtured by God's grace through word and sacrament. It is served by the ordained ministry and also held together by other bonds of communion.[16]

Clearly this suggests that any full consideration of the goal of 'full visible unity' involves not only attention to matters of the practices or order of the Church, but also to some central dogmatic conceptions. In the rest of these remarks, I want to open up three such issues for reflection.

points for discussion

1. First, some remarks on each term in the notion of 'full visibility'. The way in which the visible unity to which we aspire is qualified as *full* sets the dominant Anglican position apart from the model of unity as 'reconciled diversity', as well as from one interpretation of the Nairobi notion of 'conciliar fellowship'. The 'reconciled diversity' model, which has been attractive to at least some Lutheran theologians, takes various forms, all of which envisage the unity of the Church as that of a fellowship which allows for some measure of diversity expressed in structural forms. Such forms might include, for example, distinct denominational or confessional identities. These continuing diversities within the one Church would be balanced by the existence of structures of fellowship or communion to enable common action, witness and worship. 'Reconciled diversity' has not commended itself to the mainstream Anglican ecumenical ethos (worries about it have often been articulated by Mary Tanner); Anglicans have often urged that the continued co-existence of confessionally distinct congregations or denominations is, in fact, fatal to unity, and leaves the real scandal of disunity untouched. In effect, reconciled diversity is considered a concession to disunity and a compromise with the present realities of friendly consultation without real structural unity. Much of the criticism of 'reconciled diversity' may be correct. It can all too easily lead the Churches to heave a great sigh of relief that ecumenical reconciliation will not prove so invasive or so costly as might be feared. Moreover, the American Lutheran ecumenist Michael Root may have a point when he suggests – *contra* many of his Lutheran colleagues – that 'reconciled diversity' is too close to friendly competition in the religious marketplace for comfort.[17] Even if reconciled diversity be thought of simply as a stage on the way to full, visible unity, it is not quite clear how much reconciliation is required for Churches to be reconciled: presumably reconciliation has to be a bit more than just calling a truce. On the other hand, however, we should not forget that part of what attracts Anglicans to the notion of 'full' visible unity is that it is a way of keeping the historic episcopate on the table as one of the conditions for reunion.

This much is clear, I believe, from the way in which the notion of full, visible unity has unfolded over the last couple of decades, and from the way in which Anglicans have tended to gloss wider ecumenical notions like 'visible communion' and 'full communion' in such a way as to make clear that the qualifier *full* also refers to non-negotiable commitments to a certain understanding of the ministry of oversight.

What of the term 'visible'? Anglican ecumenism has characteristically been heavily committed to the tangible, historical and material character of the Church as an ordered society. In this, of course, it reflects not only a principal strand of interpretation of Anglicanism which has deeply valued the ordered life of the Church, but also the general consensus in ecumenical ecclesiology that the notion of the invisibility of the Church has little to commend it. Talk of the invisibility of the Church suggests a spiritualizing of the Church into bare subjectivism without much by way of objective social form or durability; and it coheres ill with the character of the Church as sign or sacrament, that is, with the emphasis on the *externality* of the Church in a good deal of modern ecclesiology. And because the Anglican tradition of ecumenical work has been deeply shaped by the consciences of those with strong commitments to a particular rendering of catholic order, this emphasis on visibility or externality has proved especially appealing.

In this context, the crucial question is not *whether* the Church is visible, but: what *kind* of visibility? Clearly a conception of the Church in which the wrong kind of invisibility predominates will not give us much purchase on the Church as a political society, and to that extent will not prove particularly helpful in advancing the structural reconciliation of the Churches. But to say that is simply to reinforce the need for explication of what is involved in talking of the visibility of the Church. Without that sort of explication, we will be likely to assume an account of the matter by default. Moreover, without it we may miss the beat of what our ecumenical conversation partners are saying to us because we assume that – for example – their rejection of *our* notion of visibility is a rejection of *any* notion of visibility (this has sometimes happened in conversation with Lutherans). A good deal hangs, therefore, on careful specification of the nature of the visibility of the Church which is the goal of ecumenism; only such specification can yield us criteria by which to evaluate progress. In a very helpful phrase, André Birmelé suggests that there is a 'scale of visibility' on which we may plot different ecclesiologies and ecumenical strategies.[18] I am not yet sure whether Birmelé is right to suggest that different Anglican bilaterals are to be placed at different points on the scale (he sees a difference between Porvoo and Meissen, and between Anglican–Lutheran and Anglican–Reformed strategies). But it is clear that the Church of England needs to be very self-aware about how it conceives of the visibility of the Church, and of other dogmatic accounts implied or explicated by its ecumenical conversation partners. One of the core issues emerging at the Second Meissen Theological Conference was precisely this issue, notably in Ingolf Dalferth's paper on 'Ministry and the Office of Bishop', which subjects Meissen and Porvoo to rather fierce critique on the matter from the standpoint of a different theology of visibility.[19] In short: our account of the goal of ecumenism is only as good as the account of the Church's visibility which undergirds it.

My own – entirely unofficial – suggestion is that for a host of historical and theological reasons Anglicans have routinely overplayed an understanding of visibility which associates it too strictly with ordered externality, and underplayed what that stout ecumenist Karl Barth called the 'very special visibility' of the Church.[20] By that, Barth did not intend to deny that the Church of Jesus Christ has concrete, historical form; he simply sought to affirm that the Church has visible form by virtue of the presence and action of Jesus Christ through the Holy Spirit; and he wanted to deny that any contingent historical ordering could guarantee or ensure the essence of the Church, since to say that would be to pass the Church from the hands of its Lord to the hands of its human members. Visibility is thus a spiritual event, describable only by talk of the presence and action of God, and not convertible without residue into forms. Again, this is not a denial of externality, but an attempt to spell out how the Church's externality is a function of present divine action, of which the externality of the Church is a witness. Hence the principle: 'The visible attests the invisible'[21] – 'invisible' meaning 'spiritually visible', perceptible by faith in the work of God. Perhaps the most crucial bit of dogmatic work which Anglicans need to undertake here is to spell out full, visible unity in such a way that the necessary concrete *forms* of unity (apostolic confession, common sacraments and ministry, and *episcope*) can credibly be shown to attest the invisible rather than replace the invisible with contingent structures or order.

2. What I have said about the Church's visibility relates to a more general dogmatic question concerning the place of the Church in the divine economy of salvation, and, by derivation, the centrality of ecclesiology to ecumenical theological discussion. One of the most striking features of current doctrinal theology is the quite extraordinary way in which ecclesiology has become 'first theology',

that is, doctrinally basic. One could trace this not only in contemporary Roman Catholic and Anglican ecclesiologies, but also in Lutherans like Lindbeck and Jenson, Free Church theologians like Volf, right through to the pan-eucharistic metaphysics of *Radical Orthodoxy* (a book whose title is a textbook example of catachresis). There is a great deal here which demands full discussion; but one comment may serve to indicate some of the issues.

One rarely noticed feature of current ecclesiology is the rather slight role played by the theology of the Word, notably in the *koinonia* ecclesiology in which Anglican ecumenics has invested so heavily. By 'Word' in this context I do not refer primarily to Holy Scripture; rather, I use the term to refer to the gratuitous, transcendent, communicative presence of God in the prophetic ministry of the risen Christ who, through the Spirit, distributes the benefits of his saving work. One of the crucial effects of deploying a theology of the Word in this sense in ecclesiology is to highlight the Church's dependence upon the free grace of God. In pointing to the sheer gratuity of the origin and life of the Church, a fundamental *distinction* is drawn between the personal divine saving action and the life of the Church. That is, where *koinonia* ecclesiologies emphasize participation, Word ecclesiologies stress difference. There is, of course, a continuum here, not a simple antithesis: it is quite possible to develop a theological account of the fellowship between God and humanity which respects difference, and to have a theology of the Word which is rooted in the bond of life between God and the Church (Calvin is a good example of both).[22] If Anglican documents have not demonstrated much interest in making these kind of refinements, it is largely because they have followed the trend of *koinonia* ecclesiologies in espousing with a rather smooth sense of the continuity between the *opus Dei* and the activities and forms (especially the ministerial forms) of the Church. It is a worry on this score which, I suspect, is the real heart of the *non placet* of those Lutherans who lament the lack of a theology of the Word in the notion of visible unity. Their protest is not against sacrament or ministry, but against what they take to be a thin theology of the immediate presence and activity of Christ in the Spirit, which they fear is compromised by the kind of emphasis on order and sacrament they find in some ecumenical ecclesiology.[23] At the very least, this means that if we are to reassure our conversation partners of the doctrinal defensibility of our conception of the goal of ecumenism, Anglicans need to give attention to the Christology and pneumatology which underlie our model of visible unity. I remain personally unconvinced about the viability of the deeper dogmatic foundations of that model; others may be easier to please, but the matter needs making explicit. Again: our account of the visibility of the Church will be only as good as the Christology and pneumatology which undergird it.

3. A third, related, issue concerns the eschatological aspects of commitment to full visible unity as our ecumenical goal. The eschatological relativization of unity is certainly given some stress in recent documents.

> Perfect unity must await the final coming of God's Kingdom, where all will be completely obedient to God and therefore totally reconciled to one another in God . . . All our attempts to describe this vision are bound to be provisional. We are continually being led to see fresh depths and riches of that unity, and to grasp new ways in which it might be manifested in word and life. Every experience of unity is a gift of God and a foretaste and sign of the Kingdom.[24]

But we might ask ourselves exactly what role is played here by eschatology. The suggestion appears to be that unity is an eschatological goal, not to be perfectly realized in history, but that each step we take towards full, visible unity is a move towards perfection (foretaste not emetic). Eschatology perfects, but does not erase or overthrow, our current ecclesial and ecumenical projects. But is this incremental eschatology all that needs to be said? Some of our conversation partners might be tempted to read what we say as putting most of the burden of change on them: the full, visible unity which will be ours in heaven looks rather more like our current set-up than theirs, and we therefore seem to be a bit more on target for the eschatological goal. I remember a Lutheran–Anglican discussion in Ontario shortly after *The Niagara Report* came out, at which the Lutheran bishops lamented the fact that the changes which they were asked to make were hopelessly disproportionate to what was asked of Anglicans (see *The Niagara Report*, paragraphs 81–110). Doctrinally, this raises deep questions about the perfection of the Church, and especially about the relation between the provisionality of the Church and apparently non-negotiable character of certain forms of visibility. Practically it raises questions about the place of the ecumenical virtue of forbearance,[25] and about the place of repentance. Gillian Evans suggests that one of the lessons of the last century of ecumenical work is that 'We have to see that we may have been wrong and acknowledge that others have been right'.[26] What theology of the visibility of the Church fits best with such a commitment? And how might it shape our account of the ecumenical goal?

chapter two

symphonic discord: the place of diversity in unity statements

Peter Fisher

The language of harmony and symphony comes readily to ecumenical writers. What, after all, is the hope of those who work for Christian unity other than that all those who follow Christ should live together in the spirit of 'truth, unity and *concord*'?

Harmony, by definition, involves the conjunction of different pitches of voice or sound. So the musical analogy helps to express a vital commitment of the modern ecumenical movement: that unity should not equate with uniformity but should embrace appropriate diversity. But some different pitches do not fit comfortably together in harmony: they 'clash', as we say. So, is there a place for discord in this business of theological composition? And at what point is it right to judge that discord, or diversity of Christian belief or practice, has the effect of spoiling the symphony, making of it something we do not recognize as music at all? In musical terms, these questions would yield different answers in different ages and different cultures. But the Christian theologian looks for durable ways of understanding the relationships and tensions that are implied by the two words 'unity' and 'diversity', ways that fit with the witness of Holy Scripture and the first century as much as with the world of ecumenism and the twenty-first century. Here, then, is a fundamental issue for all who seek Christian unity.

This chapter offers a review of recent statements and reports of ecumenical dialogues involving representatives of the Church of England, along with some related literature. This review is firstly an exercise in analysis and taxonomy, with the aim of clarifying the ways in which this issue has been dealt with in ecumenical documents. Secondly, it raises the question of consistency as between different documents and different models. Thirdly, it ventures some critical and constructive comments.

Examination of this range of documents shows that the relationship of unity and diversity is a less prominent issue than might be expected in the reports of recent ecumenical conversations. There are a number of partial exceptions to this generalization: the Fetter Lane Common Statement (from the Anglican–Moravian conversations), the Anglican–Reformed International Commission's report, *God's Reign and Our Unity*, and the ARCIC statement *Life in Christ*.

In what follows, Part I sets out some brief preliminary considerations, Part II outlines a schema of ways of dealing with the relationship of Unity and Diversity, Part III surveys the documents with reference to this schema and Part IV offers some conclusions.

I preliminary considerations

- The documents reviewed here originate in differing circumstances. Not only are the 'conversation partners' different, the size and extent of the dialogue group may also differ, the duration of the process may differ, the *modus operandi* adopted may differ, the form and style of the published document or documents may differ.[1] It is important to avoid interpreting the products of these differences as, necessarily, inconsistencies in theological method.

- Some of the documents reviewed here are from conversations now discontinued,[2] either on account of 'success' (e.g. Meissen, Fetter Lane) or 'failure' (e.g. *Proposals for a Covenant*); others are still continuing. Some questions arise here. How do inconsistencies of method relate to the 'failure' or 'success' of conversations? How far do we allow for the fact that method may validly evolve over time, that new approaches may supersede the old? Equally, is there a danger that methods adopted in 'failed' conversations may be ignored and neglected?

- The climate of thought and life within which these dialogues occur is constantly changing. How does this general observation bear on the specific concern of this chapter? It may be that concepts such as 'consensus', or even 'unity' itself, were viewed less sceptically in post-war Europe than in the global context of present-day ecumenism, with less consciousness of the spectre of oppression. It would not be surprising (or wrong?) if a concern for the defence of diversity was seen to emerge particularly in more recent documents.

- There is a useful distinction to be drawn between *diachronic* and *synchronic* diversity (i.e. diversity *over extended time* and diversity *at any one given time*). The phrase 'unity and diversity' tends to be employed in relation to synchronic diversity, and the recognition and reconciliation of differences between Churches *as they now are* is bound to be the primary focus of ecumenical theology. But the resolution of issues relating to historic or diachronic diversity is also important, not least because growth in unity involves the healing of memories. If that healing is to be more than simply 'letting bygones be bygones', it must mean the honest identification both of past divergences between traditions and of different attitudes to history within particular traditions.[3] The Introduction to *An Anglican–Methodist Covenant* gives closer attention than other documents both to the historic relationships of the two communities and to the 'myths' and 'stereotypes' which have coloured the interpretation of those relationships.[4]

- Since ecumenical conversations have to do with ecclesiology, they must inevitably operate in the borderland where doctrinal statements and the observations and interests of the human sciences overlap and interact. Some approaches to unity and diversity are particularly sensitive to issues of identity, culture and 'ethos' among our Churches.[5] Where these issues arise there is no given or agreed understanding as to how the social and theological domains should relate. Indeed, the very assumption that matters of culture and identity influence the character and concerns of Christian communities is as alien to some Churches as it appears undeniable to others.

- It has been well remarked that some shades of opinion and theology are under-represented or unrepresented in ecumenical conversations. This is typically the case with the evangelical wings of (for instance) the Anglican and Methodist Churches. Some 'Common Statements' leave a question hanging in the air as to whether their agreement really includes these shades of opinion. It follows that, within any one tradition, there may be more diversity than the ecumenical consensus is prone to recognize.

II some ways of dealing with issues of unity and diversity

Before surveying the relevant statements it is worth pausing a little longer to review a number of distinctive approaches to unity and diversity. The categorization that follows is artificial, in the sense that it separates out gambits which practitioners of ecumenical dialogue tend to interweave. Nor does the list exhaust the range of theoretical possibilities, rather it represents those that figure in the documents under review.

1. Many statements assert that not all diversity is problematic, or incompatible with true unity. Thus a simple distinction is commonly drawn between 'legitimate' and 'illegitimate' diversity. Some criteria may lie behind this distinction, but these are often not stated or are only hinted at by the use of the parallel phrase 'non-divisive and divisive' or of the expression 'differences . . . not serious enough to divide our Churches'.[6]

   This may be an important assertion to make in the abstract, but the distinction is difficult to clarify or tease out without reference to particular instances. In certain cases (e.g. the Fetter Lane Common Statement; the ARCIC statement *Life in Christ*) agreed statements have begun to put flesh on the bones of the distinction.

2. In some statements diversity is viewed as the product of historical divergence, whereby the Churches have 'gone their separate ways'. This seems to be implied by Pope John Paul II's characterization of the methodology of ARCIC as, 'going behind the habit of thought and expression born and nourished in enmity and controversy, to scrutinize together the great common treasure'.[7] Such approaches will necessarily be subject to interrogation by historical scholarship.

3. Unity and diversity may be defined as twin attributes properly belonging to the *koinonia* ('communion' or 'fellowship') of the Church. In more recent statements, especially following the publication of the Canberra Declaration of 1991 (cited in the Appendix, below) this *koinonia* is seen as rooted in the 'unity and diversity of the Godhead'. However, whilst many statements use the language of *koinonia* to suggest a link between the doctrine of the Trinity and the fellowship of the Church, not all make the link specifically in terms of 'unity and diversity'.[8]

4. Diversity may be allowed for or validated by invoking a hierarchy or gradation of truth or importance. Thus, diversity may be allowed in [a] 'non-fundamentals' whilst unity is preserved in 'fundamentals', or agreement about [b] 'essentials' may be maintained along with diversity in 'matters indifferent' or *adiaphora*. A rather different twist is given to the same syntactical form when [c] different 'derived conclusions' are seen to be drawn from 'the same underlying (or fundamental) values'.[9]

5. In one document (*God's Reign and Our Unity*), the concept of the 'provisional' nature of the Church in time, relative to the finality of the *eschaton*, is seen as a key to the need for diversity. In implied contrast to the perfect unity which will characterize the community of the *eschaton*, the life of the Church now, 'must, if it is to be true to its nature, neither destroy this diversity by the imposition of a false and premature unity which pretends to embody what will only be truly known at the end; nor absolutize the diverse elements by allowing them to destroy the unity which is Christ's gift'.[10]

6. Diverse practices or interpretations of belief can be viewed as complementary (with the implication – though this is seldom drawn out – that together they form some greater whole or unity). Here, reference may naturally be made [a] to 1 Corinthians 12 and the concept of diversity of gifts in one body. Similarly, several documents refer to [b] 'diverse cultural expressions' all related to a 'common goal' or basis. In more recent statements, [c] the musical analogy of 'harmony' comprised of different 'notes' or even of a 'symphony' has figured.[11]

7. Quite a different approach to these issues appears when the notion of 'rights of conscience' or 'liberty of conscience' is invoked, in other words, when diversity is viewed not so much from the perspective of the Church's need for unity as the individual Christian's claim to be 'free to differ'. This theme plays a significant part in the language of the *Proposals for a Covenant* of 1980.[12] The most recent ARCIC statement on authority in the Church, *The Gift of Authority*, also touches on the place of the conscience of the individual in relation both to the exercise and acceptance of authority in the Church.[13]

8. Common statements and the formal reports of conversations are usually succinct, so the motifs in this list are often represented only by a few words and phrases. Also, like members of a large family, they often borrow each other's clothes. The result is that it can be difficult to judge how far these brief references in a given statement represent considered or distinctive theological positions.

III survey of documents

This survey is organized chronologically, by reference to the date of the inception of formal conversations. Number references in square brackets refer to the categories in the list above (Part II).

a Appeal to all Christian People

The 'Appeal to all Christian People' issued by the Lambeth Conference of 1920 affirms in section IV that, 'It is through . . . diversity of life and devotion that the unity of the whole fellowship will be fulfilled.'

b Anglican–Orthodox dialogue

(1) The Moscow Agreed Statement of 1977 gives no explicit consideration to the issue of diversity as such; as a text it is characterized by a strong emphasis on what Cardinal Ratzinger might term 'unicity'.[14] In the section (III) on Scripture and Tradition, however, a distinction of the general character of [4a] is drawn between differing 'liturgical and canonical *expressions* of Tradition . . . concerned with the varying situations of the people of God' and the 'liturgical and canonical *traditions*' which 'remain unchangeable to the extent that they embody the unchangeable truth of divine revelation and respond to the unchanging needs of mankind' (my emphases).[15]

The statement also expresses Orthodox concern about the 'comprehensiveness' of Anglicanism.

(2) The Dublin Agreed Statement of 1984 shows the marks of the struggle to sustain dialogue in the light of Anglican ordinations of women. Nonetheless, diversity as such is not a theme. The question of *difference* figures, again, in relation to the 'greater variety of attitude and teaching' allowed within the Anglican 'Church' (*sic*),[16] and in a substantive disagreement as to whether there can be division *within* the Church.[17] Under the heading 'Marks of the Church' paragraph 12, dealing with Catholicity, affirms the diversity manifested by local Churches: 'As long as their witness to the one faith remains unimpaired [1], such diversity is to be seen not as a deficiency or cause for division [8], but as a mark of the fullness of the one Spirit who distributes to each according to his will (I Cor. 12.11)' [6a].

c Anglican–Roman Catholic dialogue

The work of ARCIC I and II has stretched over more than thirty years, has involved two successive commissions and has issued in at least twelve specific texts. Consequently, some differences in style and approach may be discerned between one document and another.

At the same time, the two commissions have consciously maintained a particular approach to their task [3].

(1) ARCIC I *The Final Report*

The preparatory commission's Malta Report forms an appendix to this compilation. Whilst the characteristic notes of ARCIC method (understanding of difference as arising from historical divergence, to be 'got behind' [3]) are struck in paragraphs 3 and 4, this Report also sets out a more positive approach [8] to diversity than is to be found in many subsequent documents in the series: 'we believe that diversity has intrinsic value when used creatively rather than destructively'.[18] The following paragraph invokes the notion of a 'hierarchy of truths' from Vatican 2 [4] and cites the Decree on Ecumenism as to the complementarity of diverse theological traditions [6].[19]

The 1971 Agreed Statement on Eucharistic Doctrine includes something like an *apologia* for the absence of explicit attention to diversity: 'We acknowledge a variety of theological approaches within both our communions. But we have seen it as our task to find a way of advancing together beyond the doctrinal disagreements of the past.'[20] The ensuing *Elucidation* expresses the view [4a] that, 'Differences of theology and practice may well co-exist with a real consensus on the essentials of eucharistic faith.'[21] The notion of 'essentials' is construed in *Ministry and Ordination* (1973) in terms of 'matters where it [sc. The Commission] considers that doctrine admits no divergence'.[22] The discussion of Primacy in *Authority in the Church I* proposes a primacy which 'respects and promotes Christian freedom and spontaneity' and 'does not seek uniformity where diversity is legitimate'[23] [1]. Later, the same statement speaks of the balance between 'fruitful' or 'just' diversity [8], and unity. *Authority in the Church II* adds nothing substantial to these comments.

(2) ARCIC II

The whole 1986 statement on *Salvation and the Church* illustrates well the clear strengths and possible limitations of ARCIC methodology. Gently erasing the mutual 'caricatures' of past beliefs, the statement sketches a more balanced and inclusive portrait in which the 'essential' and best features of both are included. The whole aim is to reach 'agreement on essentials' and this precludes close consideration of abiding (or creative?) difference.

Without breaking new ground, the subsequent statement on *Church as Communion* (1991) and the 1994 study of 'Morals, Communion and the Church' (*Life in Christ*) do address the realities of diversity in the Church more closely. Diversity can be seen as a positive, enriching aspect of divine creation [8][24] and differences may form validly complementary parts of 'a living whole' [6].[25] In respect of moral teaching and discipline, 'differences there are and differences they remain' between Anglicans and Roman Catholics,[26] yet, on careful examination, these differences may be seen to be 'not on the level of fundamental moral values, but of their implementation in practical judgements' [4c].[27]

Finally, *The Gift of Authority* reserves most of its positive affirmations about diversity to one paragraph in the section about Catholicity. Citing *Church as Communion*, it asserts with more force that, 'As God has created diversity among humans, so the Church's fidelity and identity require not uniformity of expression and formulation at all levels in all situations, but rather catholic diversity within the unity of communion.' [8][28] The general tenor of the statement, however, may leave a sense that this significant paragraph is something of a 'booth in a cucumber field'.[29]

Over time, ARCIC statements have developed a confident theological style.[30] The use of what might be termed the 'dogmatic indicative' is to be found in most ecumenical reports ('The Church is a divine reality . . .', Fetter Lane; 'Christ is present and active . . . in the entire eucharistic celebration', *The Final Report*) as a natural expression of the shared assurance of the realities of the faith. It is also useful as shorthand. But while this form of expression communicates firmness and clarity to some readers, to others it communicates a sense of certitude which is in tension with the experienced reality of the fragility of the Church and of the value both of questioning and diversity within it.

d Anglican–Lutheran dialogue

Dialogue between Anglicans and Lutherans, from 1970 onwards, has been conducted in distinct phases. The 1973 report of the *Anglican–Lutheran International Conversations* is largely a mapping exercise in which differences of view are remarked without further significant comment.[31] Neither the ensuing European conversations represented in *The Helsinki Report* (1982, published 1983) nor the ALIC report on *episcope* in *The Niagara Report* (1987, published 1988) display a particular theological approach to issues of diversity.[32] These documents show more awareness of diachronic development than of synchronic diversity.[33]

The Meissen Agreement of 1988 has defined limits both of goal and participation. The text constitutes an extended preface to the joint Declaration, which the Church of England and the relevant German Evangelical Churches are called on to make. Much of the phrasing in the sections concerning the nature of the Church and of unity is drawn from the growing common stock of ecumenical language. The unity it portrays is 'grounded in the life of the Holy Trinity' [3] and will 'reflect the different gifts God has given his Church in many nations, languages, cultures and traditions'. [6] It will, 'at one and the same time respect these different gifts and manifest more fully the visibility of the one church of Jesus Christ'.[34]

The Porvoo Common Statement differs from the documents so far reviewed in the way that the notion that *episcope* 'is embodied in all our churches in a variety of forms' is put to work in its argument. The fact that, historically, *episcope* has sometimes been exercised in different ways within the signatory Churches is not held to prevent the recognition of 'the reality of the Episcopal office' or the affirmation of 'the apostolic continuity in those churches in which the sign of Episcopal succession has at some time not been used'. A more positive recognition of the place of diversity in the search for unity is entailed in this argument. Accordingly, though similar in approach to the parallel sections in Meissen, those parts of the Porvoo Statement which address diversity do so more boldly, drawing on the themes of complementarity and the gifts of the Spirit [6] and of the grounding of both unity and diversity in the 'communion of God the Holy Trinity' [2]. Diversity is 'a concept of fundamental ecclesial importance, with relevance to all aspects of the life of the Church, and not a mere concession to theological pluralism' [8].[35]

e *Proposals for a Covenant*

The 1980 report of the Churches' Council for Covenanting bears little resemblance to the other documents under scrutiny and is now, perhaps, something of a museum piece. In the terms of this study, however, its interest resides in the unique place given to 'Conscientious Reservations' [7]: 'The fullest generosity and trust is needed in respecting others' consciences and the greatest goodwill in accepting anomalies of practice as together, in conscience informed by prayer, the Covenanting Churches see that richer understanding which only together they may gain of Christ's will for his Church.'[36] The teasing task is given to 'the Churches acting together through the collegiality of the local episcopate and of national leadership to determine when these rights and reservations are asserted to the injury of their developing unity and peace or so as to negate the substance of the Covenant'.[37]

f Anglican–Reformed dialogue

God's Reign and Our Unity (1984) can be read almost as if it were a book: that is to say its style is more discursive and its approach more exploratory than other reports and statements. No doubt this reflects, at least in part, the different circumstances and expectations in which it was engendered. The report confronts the fear that large-scale organizational unity will lead to 'bureaucratically controlled uniformity' and aims to enunciate a vision of a united Church 'characterised by great diversity' like the human race itself [8]. Theologically, this is held to be grounded in the Trinity [3]: 'The pattern of unity and diversity is thus in the Godhead.'[38] The final chapter of *God's Reign* (V 'Our Goal') engages thoughtfully and extensively with the unresolved question as to 'the form that unity should take', particularly focusing on the tension between unity and diversity within an understanding of the Church as 'provisional', whilst we await the *eschaton* [5].[39] It also makes, with some care, the case for visible unity, rather than 'reconciled denominationalism' as the goal of ecumenism.

g Anglican–Moravian dialogue

Leading on from *God's Reign and Our Unity*, the Fetter Lane Common Statement of 1996 aims to set out a 'model of common life' in which the distinctive 'ethos' of both traditions is 'nurtured and shared within visible unity'[40] and in which diversity is not only permitted but encouraged and safeguarded.[41] The articulation of a theological grounding for this leans heavily and explicitly on the Canberra Declaration (see the Appendix, below).

h Anglican–French Lutheran and Reformed dialogue

The Reuilly Common Statement (*Called to Witness and Service*, 1999) expresses compactly most of the keynotes of late-twentieth-century ecumenical dialogue, welding together material from Meissen, Porvoo, the Canberra Declaration and *Facing Unity*.[42] Visible unity 'should not be confused with uniformity . . . is given with and in diversity . . . both are grounded in the Triune God' [3].[43] Touching on the limits to diversity, the statement expands on the

Canberra definition as to what makes diversity *illegitimate*. 'In communion diversities are brought together in harmony as gifts of the Holy Spirit, contributing to the richness and fullness of the Church of God.'[44]

i *An Anglican–Methodist Covenant*

The Common Statement of the formal conversations between the Methodist Church of Great Britain and the Church of England reflects the very particular history of the two partners in dialogue, a history both of close intimacy and of ecumenical disappointment and hurt. The Covenant itself is prefaced by what is, in effect, a series of quite detailed essays. This format allows for the inclusion of more historical and descriptive study of Methodism and Anglicanism than is customary in agreed statements. This has the effect of 'writing diversity in' to the story of convergence between the two, not least because it brings to light both diachronic and synchronic diversity *within* each communion as well as between the two [2]. At the same time, the clear limits of the stage of unity to which the *Covenant* is committed means that certain differences and even tensions between Methodist and Anglican practice and understanding can be acknowledged and marked as 'to be resolved at the next stage'.[45]

In its explicit references to unity and diversity, the Common Statement fills out and extends the terms of other recent statements. The value ascribed to diversity is emphatic. The aim of the process is, 'not to ... gloss over differences, and to construct a monochrome unity ... [but] to harvest our diversity, to share our treasures and to remedy our shortcomings'. The significance of diversity in the Church is placed within the context of 'Sharing in God's Mission' and, more particularly, of the Pentecostal work of the Spirit, which 'brings harmony out of discord, unity out of division.' [6] The statement continues:

> Within that divine concord there is a rich diversity. The Spirit presides over an abundance of different gifts, different stories and different identities. Diversity is cherished; it is gathered together in unity. As well as the imperative to seek unity, the Spirit gives the freedom to explore diversity (Galatians 3.28; Ephesians 4.1-16). The paradox of unity and diversity finds its resolution in the life that the Spirit gives.[46]

IV conclusions

On the evidence of this survey, the following conclusions can be drawn more or less securely.

1 **a consistent goal** In recent ecumenical dialogues the Church of England has consistently held to the goal of visible unity, however distant that goal may presently appear. Diversity has never been seen as legitimating a less ambitious goal.

2 **common affirmations** All the above documents (except the *Proposals for a Covenant*, which is framed in quite different terms) emphasize the level of agreement and unity in faith which has already been achieved and all affirm similar common requirements for visible unity.

3 **a notable exception** The Covenanting Proposals are the joker in the late twentieth-century pack of ecumenical documents. The whole methodology of its approach is so distinctive as to make other comparisons difficult. The attention given in the Proposals to the *process* whereby the Churches are called to discern the difference between appropriate and destructive manifestations of diversity finds no echo in other statements.[47] The way in which 'Unity by Stages' has been pursued in most of the dialogues under review here has led to the framing of discrete theological statements, whereas the theological affirmations in the covenanting document are made in the context of proposals that are focused on the *process* of realizing unity. This gives rise to the question, how possible is it to separate doctrinal affirmations about unity and diversity from questions about the means and processes of discernment in the Church?

The place given in the Covenanting Proposals to 'reservations of conscience' is distinctive, too. The concerns this language touches, with its implications about the relationship between the authority of the Church and the freedom of the individual, are perhaps under-represented in the 'mainstream' dialogues.[48]

4 **different partners: different emphases** There are manifest differences of character and style between the products of different dialogues. There is also evidence of a correlation between at least some of these differences and the identity of the conversational partner. Thus, the Helsinki and Dublin statements, while acknowledging differences between the emphases of Anglican and Orthodox theologies, are coloured

by a strongly eucharistic view of the Church and a stress on the unchanging essence of Tradition. Anglican–Reformed dialogue (to take another example) focuses on the Church as servant of the kingdom of God and emphasizes mission and the grace of God. The former dialogue does not dwell on the importance or potential creativity of diversity, the latter does. Is this inconsistency or ecumenical sensitivity?

5 **development through time** These divergences (3, above) must be seen in relation to historical development and change in ecumenical dialogue, for which the documents give at least some evidence. By and large, the most recent statements and reports are those which give most prominence to diversity and which endeavour to give it a positive valuation. It is not clear, however, that ARCIC II follows this trend.

6 **a distinctive Anglican perspective?** Theology in general can no longer be categorized by denomination, if it ever could be. Yet it is reasonable to expect that a particular community of faith (such as the Church of England or the Anglican Communion) should maintain a consistent and recognizable approach in conversation with other communities with distinctive Christian traditions. However, if we look for signs of such a recognizable and distinctive approach, beyond the consistent view of the goal of unity mentioned above (1), it is not easily discerned. Rather, we see on the one hand a degree of adaptability with regard to different conversation partners (4, above) and, on the other, a tendency to deploy concepts and language drawn from the 'common stock' of ecumenical phraseology which has been laid down over the last three decades. Anglican history has been much occupied with the relation of diversity and unity: the breadth and inclusiveness of the Communion has been seen as a strength and as cause of concern. In the light of this it is disappointing that little by way of a distinctive contribution to ecumenical work in this area can be detected in the documents reviewed here.

7 **the common stock of ecumenical phraseology** The community of those engaged in ecumenical conversations operates, in one regard, like a large family in which there is a good deal of borrowing and passing-on of clothes. Formulations (such as those of the Canberra Declaration) once arrived at are reused and adapted many times over. This marks a natural cumulative process by which one form of accord builds on another and it avoids the constant reinvention of the

theological wheel. But there are dangers in the frequent use of rehearsed or 'off-the-shelf' language-counters, expressions which may become invested with an accrued authority by dint of repetition. There is the risk that these forms of expression become normative in certain ecumenical circles whilst remaining obscure or unconvincing outside them. There is the risk that the process of genuine reception and re-reception by the Churches at large falls into abeyance. There is the risk that theological exploration is abandoned.

8 *Koinonia* **ecclesiology** This study has revealed the extent to which certain theological keynotes have come to prominence in recent decades of dialogue, particularly the notion that the true pattern of unity and diversity in the Church is grounded in the nature of the Triune God. The publication of John Zizioulas's seminal book, *Being as Communion*,[49] in 1985 marked the beginning of a vigorous renaissance in Trinitarian theology, within the Churches of the Western world at least. More specifically, this book encouraged the trend to link the doctrine of the Church to the doctrine of the Trinity.[50] There is space here only for a brief discussion of this important matter,[51] focusing not on the wider questions about Trinitarian theology so much as on their particular implications for an ecumenical understanding of diversity.

Put aphoristically, it may be said that much of the diversity which marks the Church on earth arises precisely because it is *not* divine, not triumphant but 'militant here on earth'. And to offer a divine model for the relationship of unity and diversity in the Church can have the unintended effect of disguising and misrepresenting the real nature of this diversity. The notional distinctions within the Trinity, however we may characterize them, cannot be viewed as examples of differences of culture, tradition or interpretation, nor as tokens of a self-identity that fears loss of itself, still less as embroiled in dispute or controversy.[52] But diversity in the earthly communities of the Church is of precisely these kinds and, precisely because of this, difficult to harmonize or unify. Consequently, when it comes to dealing with diversity in the Church the Trinitarian model of *koinonia* presents a model which is of limited value because it bears little relation to the known reality. As such, it shares in the general character of theoretical, 'blueprint' views of the Church which have been critiqued by Nicholas Healy as fostering a 'disjunction . . . between ideal ecclesiology and the realities of the concrete church'.[53]

9 **limits of 'diversity'** The word 'diversity' is called on to stand for a host of things, themselves diverse. Behind it lie the actualities of difference in teaching, in liturgy, in church order, in spirituality, in moral and political commitment, in heritage and in style. Because of the holistic imperative of Christian life, few or none of these can be divorced one from another. So a bow of the head, or its refusal, is linked with a view of liturgy, history and doctrine. The temptation offered by the word 'diversity' is to imagine all these interconnected yet disparate features as 'colours of the rainbow', more naturally combined than separated. Yet they are also entwined in debates, arguments and conflicts as to the character and interpretation of the Faith. Some of these are antique debates which have left the 'colours' of a particular tradition displayed like fading relics in contemporary churches. But others are live issues and involve kinds of discord that cannot be simply harmonized with integrity. In the struggle for unity both *within* and *between* Churches these forms of diversity rooted in unresolved difference need to be treated with full seriousness.

Nor need these seemingly problematic aspects of diversity be seen only as 'impairing unity'. Judging by the record of the New Testament and the history of the Church, such tensions and disputes have been essential to the Church's exploration of the gospel, to finding out what Christians should believe and do in each new age.[54] It may be that if ecumenical theology accepts more realistically the *exploratory* implications of the nature of the Church as a 'pilgrim people', more robust and serviceable models of unity and diversity will be forged.

10 **summary** The evidence of this survey indicates that, whilst there are differences of emphasis in this area between different statements, a predominant approach has emerged with respect to the relation of unity and diversity. This approach draws on the notions of complementarity, harmony and *koinonia* and suggests that some forms of diversity are proper to the nature of the Church and rooted in the nature of God the Holy Trinity. This approach needs further theological exploration and critique. It too easily sidesteps the uncomfortable reality of 'discord' within and between the Churches. In doing so it has the unintended effect of making ecumenical documents seem out of touch with reality, given the prominence of public disagreements among contemporary Christians. More importantly, perhaps, it may blind us to the contribution *dis*harmony can make to the entire symphony.

Appendix

From the Canberra Declaration: *The Unity of the Church as Koinonia: Gift and Calling* 2.2

> Diversities which are rooted in theological traditions, various cultural, ethnic or historical contacts are integral to the nature of communion; yet there are limits to diversity. Diversity is illegitimate when, for instance, it makes impossible the common confession of Jesus Christ as God and Saviour, the same yesterday, today and forever (Heb 13.8); and salvation and the final destiny of humanity as proclaimed in holy scripture and preached by the apostolic community. In communion diversities are brought together in harmony as gifts of the Holy Spirit, contributing to the richness and fullness of the church of God.

Cited from M. Kinnamon (ed.), *Signs of the Spirit*, WCC Publications, 1991, p. 173.

chapter three

Anglican ecumenism: the Liberal Catholic consensus and the Conservative Evangelical challenge

Martin Davie

1. official ecumenical policy

Canon A 8 of the Canons of the Church of England declares that:

> Forasmuch as the Church of Christ has for a long time past been distressed by separations and schisms among Christian men, so that the unity for which our Lord prayed is impaired and the witness to his gospel is grievously hindered, it is the duty of clergy and people to do their utmost not only to avoid occasions of strife but also to seek in penitence and brotherly charity to heal such divisions.

Given this canonical declaration of the importance of the promotion of Christian unity we would expect to find the Church of England actively involved in the work of the ecumenical movement, and this is, indeed, exactly what we do find.

According to the *Church of England Year Book*: 'The Church of England is committed to the search for full visible unity with other Christian Churches, and to the bodies which promote this at the local, intermediate, national, European and world levels.'[1] If the term 'Church of England' in this quotation means the Church of England as an institution, then this statement is certainly true, and has been for very many years. As G. K. A. Bell explains in his book *Christian Unity – the Anglican Position*,[2] the issue of the relationship between the Church of England and other Christian Churches is one that has concerned members of the Church of England from the Reformation onwards, and since the end of the nineteenth century the Church of England as an institution has been actively involved in the search for full visible unity with other Christian

Churches and has taken a full part in the work of a wide range of ecumenical organizations.

At the Lambeth Conference of 1888 the bishops of the Church of England, together with the other bishops of the Anglican Communion, adopted what has become known as the Chicago–Lambeth Quadrilateral as 'a basis on which approach may be by God's blessing made towards home reunion'. The Quadrilateral consists of four 'articles' which the conference saw as necessary for a reunited Church:

- The Holy Scriptures of the Old and New Testaments, as 'containing all things necessary to salvation', and as being the rule and ultimate standard of faith;

- The Apostles' Creed as the baptismal symbol; and the Nicene Creed, as the sufficient statement of the Christian faith;

- The two sacraments ordained by Christ himself – Baptism and the Supper of the Lord – ministered with unfailing use of Christ's words of institution, and of the elements ordained by him;

- The historic episcopate, locally adapted in the methods of its administration to the varying needs of the nations and peoples called of God into the unity of the Church.

At the Lambeth Conference of 1920 the Church of England, together with the other Churches of the Anglican Communion, issued an Appeal to all Christian People to work for the visible unity of the Church. This declared:

> The time has come . . . we believe, for all the separated groups of Christians to agree in forgetting the things that are behind and reaching out towards the goal of a reunited Catholic Church. The removal of the barriers which have arisen between them will only be brought about by a new comradeship of those whose faces are definitely set this way.[3]

The Appeal continued:

> The vision which rises before us is that of a Church, genuinely Catholic, loyal to all truth, and gathering into its fellowship all 'who profess and call themselves Christians' within whose visible unity all the treasures of faith and order, bequeathed as a heritage by the past to the present, shall be possessed in common, and made serviceable to the whole body of Christ. Within this unity Christian Communions now separate from one another would retain much that has long been distinctive in their methods of life and service. It is through a rich diversity

of life and devotion that the unity of the whole fellowship will be fulfilled.[4]

As in 1888, the basis proposed for such unity is a common acceptance of the Bible, the Nicene and Apostles' Creeds, the two sacraments of baptism and the Holy Communion, and an episcopal ministry.

Furthermore, the Church of England has not only appealed for unity. It has also taken action to promote the visible unity of the Church on the basis of the principles set out in the Lambeth Appeal in a whole series of bilateral and multilateral dialogues with Churches from the Roman Catholic, Old Catholic, Orthodox, Lutheran, Reformed, Moravian, Baptist and Methodist traditions and with the Free Church of England.

As a result of this ecumenical activity, the Church of England has been in communion with the Old Catholic Churches since the Bonn Agreement of 1931 and is in communion with certain of the Nordic and Baltic Lutheran Churches on the basis of the Porvoo Common Satement of 1992. In addition, the Church of England is in communion with the United Churches of South India, North India, Pakistan, Bangladesh and Ceylon (Sri Lanka), and the Meissen Agreement of 1991, the Fetter Lane Common Statement of 1995 and the Reuilly Common Statement of 1999 have committed the Church of England to working towards full visible unity with the Evangelical Church in Germany, the Moravian Church of Great Britain and Ireland and the Lutheran and Reformed Churches of France.

As well as taking part in the bilateral and multilateral negotiations, there was Church of England representation on the pre-war Universal Christian Conference on Life and Work and the World Conference on Faith and Order, and the Church of England has been a member of the World Council of Churches, the Council of European Churches and the British Council of Churches and its successor, the Council of Churches for (now Churches Together in) Britain and Ireland since their inception.

There is thus clear and incontrovertible evidence that the Church of England as an institution has been consistently involved in the search for the full visible unity of the Church, and has taken concrete steps to move towards this unity. Furthermore, not only has there been a consistency of purpose, but there has also been a consistency of principle and a developing consistency of method.

The consistency of principle lies in the fact that underlying the Church of England's official attitude towards church unity has been a belief that the unity of the Church must consist not only in the spiritual unity of believers through their common union with Christ, but also in the outward expression of that unity in a common form of ecclesiastical organization along the lines laid down in the Lambeth Appeal. That is what has been meant by the use of the term 'full visible unity'.

The developing consistency of method has emerged as the Church of England has engaged in the dialogues noted above and has had to think about how a movement towards full visible unity between the Church of England and other Churches could take place. The solution that has been arrived at has been based on a distinction between 'recognition' and 'reconciliation'. 'Recognition' has come to mean an acceptance that there is sufficient agreement on faith and practice between the Church of England and some other Church for the Church of England to be able to recognize that other Church as a true part of the One, Holy, Catholic and Apostolic Church. 'Reconciliation', on the other hand, has come to mean the achievement of a structural unity between the Church of England and some other Church based on the development of a commonly agreed form of oversight and a commonly agreed form of episcopally ordained ministry.

As the Reuilly Common Statement puts it:

> Anglicans . . . make a distinction between the recognition (acknowledgement) of the Church of Christ in another tradition, including the authentic word, sacraments and ministries of the other churches, and a further stage – the formation of a reconciled, common ministry in the historic episcopal succession, together with the establishment of collegial and conciliar oversight.[5]

On the institutional level, therefore, the Church of England's attitude to matters ecumenical is extremely straightforward and easy to describe. The Church of England is committed to the attainment of full visible unity, it has a clear understanding of what the requirements for full visible unity are, and it has developed a clear method of approach to the problem of how to move towards this goal.

However, what also needs to be noted is that the Church of England's attitude to ecumenism is only clear and straightforward at the institutional level. Closer examination shows that there have been, and still are, significant differences between members of the Church of England on a number of important issues to do with ecumenism: the nature of the Church's unity; the importance of the episcopate; how a reunited Church might be achieved; and the place of the papacy in a reunited Church.

2. the nature of the Church's unity

As I have already explained, the goal of official Anglican ecumenical activity has been the development of the outward and visible unity of the Church through the emergence of a common ecclesiastical polity with a commonly agreed form of episcopal ministry.

The belief in the visible and organizational nature of the Church's unity, and the importance of episcopal ministry, which has inspired this approach to ecumenism is one that was shared by many Church of England theologians during the course of the last century.

Four examples will serve to illustrate this point.

My first example is from a commentary on the Thirty-Nine Articles by E. J. Bicknell, for long a standard textbook for ordinands in the Catholic tradition. In the third edition of this textbook the commentary on Article XIX notes that there exists a serious line of division between Catholic and Protestant understandings of the Church's unity:

> The continuity of historical and sacramental life, which to the 'catholic' is embodied in the continuity of the episcopate and is one important aspect of the continual abiding of the Church in Christ, is unintelligible to the 'protestant' who finds continuity in the faithful acceptance and preaching of God's word and believes that a group or body of Christians which is faithful in this way may legitimately set up its own form of ministry. For this and other reasons there is no general agreement as to the shape of the visible unity towards which Christians should move. 'Organic unity' is by no means universally accepted as its proper description.[6]

Having made this point, the commentary then goes on to claim that the Anglican Communion has adopted the Catholic approach to this matter:

> Through its Bishops assembled in successive Lambeth Conferences the Anglican Communion has made clear its desire and intention to take a full part in the work for unity.

The traditional order of ecclesiastical life with its emphasis on
the sacraments and the threefold ministry, which we have
inherited and maintained, makes it impossible for us to regard
the visible unity of the Church as of secondary importance. We
have consistently maintained that this unity will not be reached
without the general acceptance, as its basis, of the scriptures,
the faith of the Nicene Creed, the sacraments of Baptism and
Holy Communion, and the episcopate with its historic functions
and continuity.[7]

For Bicknell, church unity is not simply an invisible spiritual reality,
but an outward and visible matter manifested not only in theological
and sacramental unity, but in the common acceptance of an
episcopal form of ministry. In similar fashion, Michael Ramsey
argues in his classic essay *The Gospel and the Catholic Church*
that the outward order of the Church is a matter of critical
theological importance because it manifests the gospel message
of death to self and resurrection to a new form of common life
in the body of Christ:

the good news that God has visited and redeemed His people
includes the redeemed man's knowledge of death and
resurrection through his place in the one visible society and
through the death to self in which every member and group
has died. And in telling of this one visible society the Church's
outward order tells indeed of the Gospel. For every part of the
Church's true order will bear witness to the one universal family
of God and will point to the historic events of the Word-made-
flesh. Thus Baptism is into the death and resurrection of Christ,
and into the one Body (Rom 6.3, 1 Cor 12.13); the Eucharist
is likewise a sharing in Christ's death and the merging of the
individual into the one Body (1 Cor 11.26, 1 Cor 10.17); and
the Apostles are both a link with the historical Jesus and also
the officers of the one ecclesia whereon every local community
depends. Hence the whole structure of the Church tells of the
Gospel; not only by its graces and virtues, but also by its mere
organic shape it proclaims the truth. A Baptism, a Eucharistic
service, an Apostle, in themselves tell us of our death and
resurrection and of the Body that is one.[8]

Having emphasized the role of the apostles in the Church's outward
order, Ramsey subsequently goes on to claim that the function of
the apostle in the New Testament Church is continued by the
subsequent office of bishop with the corollary that for the Church
today the maintenance of episcopacy is essential if the Church is

to properly express the gospel in its corporate life. For Ramsey, therefore, the very nature of the gospel entails the necessity for the existence of a common form of outward church order involving the ministry of bishops.

My third example of this way of looking at the unity of the Church comes from A. C. Headlam's 1920 Bampton lectures *The Doctrine of the Church and Reunion*. Towards the end of these lectures Headlam sets out what he thinks the reunion of the Church requires and declares that:

> Christ ordained two Sacraments – Baptism and the Communion of His Body and Blood – and instituted a ministry for His Church. These Sacraments, therefore, and such a ministry are necessary for His Church. In the present divided and imperfect state of the Church all those who celebrate the Sacraments according to the command of our Lord and with the full intention of fulfilling His will, and who appoint their ministers as His Apostles did with prayer and the laying on of hands, must be held to have valid Sacraments and Orders; but to create a united Church, which shall be a real organic union, we must follow that which became the universal rule of the whole Church, and is even now accepted by the vast majority of Christians, and accept the traditional ministry of Episcopacy and episcopal ordinations, and administer these in a careful and orderly way.[9]

My fourth and final example comes from John Macquarrie's well-known textbook *Principles of Christian Theology*. At the end of the section in which he discusses the four classic credal 'notes' of the Church, Macquarrie writes as follows:

> As an actual historical association, the Church exhibits 'more or less' the unity, holiness, catholicity, and apostolicity which will fully belong to it only when it gives itself up in order to become the kingdom of God. It exhibits unity the more it is obedient to Christ as its head; holiness, the more the divine Spirit is immanent and active within it; catholicity and apostolicity, the more it manifests the authentic Christian faith that brings men into community across the barriers of geography, race, culture, or even time. Because it is embodied in an earthly existence, the Church has its treasures in earthen vessels that are not to be despised, and we have listed as the four most vital to it: the Holy Scriptures, the sacraments, the catholic creeds, and the historic episcopate.

The reader will have noticed that the four institutional forms or embodiments mentioned as expressing and supporting the four fundamental notes of the Church are identical with the four points put forward in the nineteenth century as the *sine qua non* for a reunion of the Church, in the so-called 'Chicago–Lambeth Quadrilateral'. This still remains the basic minimum required for any possible reunion.[10]

The first two writers from whom I have just quoted are Anglo-Catholics and the second two are leading representatives of Liberal or 'Broad Church' Anglicanism. This reflects the fact that the approach to Christian unity which the Church of England has followed reflects a broad consensus on this issue between Anglicans of Anglo-Catholic and Liberal churchmanship. It is the existence of this consensus that has allowed official Anglican ecumenical policy to develop as it has.

Many Evangelicals, particularly those of a more 'liberal' or 'open' variety, have also shared in this consensus, as can be shown with reference to individuals such as Stephen Neill, Max Warren, Julian Charley and the present chairman of the Church of England's Council for Christian Unity, Bishop Ian Cundy. However, the conservative end of the Evangelical Anglican spectrum has also produced dissenting voices which have advocated a variety of alternative approaches to unity.

This fact can be clearly seen if one looks at the view of unity taken by three representative conservative Evangelical writers. They put forward a variety of approaches to what church unity is about, but, unlike the four writers referred to above, none of them concurs with the approach that the Church of England has followed.

My first Evangelical example is from W. H. Griffith Thomas's work *The Principles of Theology*, a commentary on the Articles of Religion which was first published in 1931 and was for many years the Evangelical alternative to Bicknell. Commenting on Article XIX, Griffith Thomas argues that the Church's unity is a spiritual rather than an organizational unity:

> What is the meaning of Unity? (1) Not unanimity of opinion. That is clear from the New Testament itself. There was essential unity in the midst of much difference of opinion. (2) Not uniformity of usages. This was not part of the early Church, as the four families of Liturgies clearly show. (3) Not a unit of organisation. This has not existed since the first congregation in Jerusalem. There is no such unit in the East to-day, where

there is a federation of several independent and self-governing Churches. There is no such unit in the Anglican Communion, the highest point being that of the province with each Bishop the equal of the rest. Even the Archbishop of Canterbury is only primus inter pares, and it is by courtesy that he has his position as leader. It is only in the Church of Rome that a unit of organisation, with the Papacy as the head, is found, and this is only possible by the exclusion of all Christians who are unwilling to submit to the Papacy. (4) True unity is that of spiritual life in Christ by the Holy Spirit. St. Paul taught two unities; one 'of the Spirit,' which is present (Eph iv. 3), and one 'of faith and knowledge,' which can only be fully realised hereafter (Eph iv. 13). The former we are to endeavour to keep; the other we are to attain to and reach in the future. To the same effect Christ distinguishes between the unity of the fold and the unity of the flock (John x.16). An organised Church is not the flock, but only one fold, so that no one community can be the Church. The truth, therefore, is not that the Church is one, but that there is one Church. Unity in New Testament times and in the sub-Apostolic age was maintained by very simple methods; (1) by hospitality between the Churches; (2) by visits of the prophets; (3) by letters. There was no formal confederation.

Unity of spiritual life is possible amid a great variety of visible organisations. St. Paul teaches the Scriptural idea of unity when he says, 'We, being many, are one body in Christ, and every one members of one another' (Rom xii. 5). This is a present fact, not a prospect. So also in Ephesians the Apostle teaches the truth in the same way as a fact, that the Church is the body of Christ, without division, absolutely one in the Divine purpose, a fact which no divisions can alter.[11]

My second Conservative Evangelical example is from A. M. Stibbs' essay 'The Unity of All in each Place', which forms part of a volume of essays entitled *All in Each Place* which was published in 1965 as an Evangelical contribution to the debate about unity stirred up by the Anglican–Methodist Conversations which were taking place at that time. In this essay Stibbs argues for local rather than denominational unity:

> The Christians who ought to realize, deepen, and express together their unity in Christ are, precisely, the Christians of each locality. There will be no new enjoyment and worthy expression of brotherly love and fellowship in Christ, not bounded, as at

present by rigid denominational limits, until believers in Christ, who live alongside each other, and yet are separated in all their distinctively Christian activity, learn to enter in a new way into the personal and frequent practice of fellowship in the Spirit with one another. The practical problem to be faced first, if we desire fuller unity among Christians in our land, is how to establish a right relation and co-operation, not between denominational blocs and their chief administrators, but between adjacent local churches and their individual members.

This is where and how our unity in Christ ought visibly and experimentally to be enjoyed – locally, by all Christians in each place. This is indeed the only way in which Christian unity can find visible corporate expression – in the place where at present we happen to be, and in relation to fellow-Christians with whom we can meet and act together . . .

The only other way to realize Christian unity is, so to speak, to do it not horizontally but vertically; that is, to recognize by faith that we are come to mount Zion, to the city of the living God, the heavenly Jerusalem, and to Christ upon the throne; and that 'in the heavenlies' we are one with the whole body, militant and triumphant, of which Christ is the head, and of which by grace we are individually members.

In contrast to this, our unity as Christians cannot in principle be realized in any proper or distinctively Christian way by saying that we are in communion either with Rome and the Pope, or with Canterbury and its archbishop, or with the headquarters of our particular denomination. For this horizontal method of realizing institutional integration is a man-made idea, which has no scriptural sanction. It tends in practice to give to the pope or the bishop, or to the central office and its officers, a significance and function which belong to Christ alone. In this connection there is both place and need for proper jealous concern for the 'crown rights' of the Redeemer.[12]

My third Evangelical example is taken from an essay entitled 'The Doctrine and Expression of Christian Unity' by the veteran Evangelical theologian J. I. Packer, which is published in his volume of essays entitled *Serving the People of God*. Packer was a member of the Anglican–Methodist conversations in the 1960s and was a member of the Church of England's Faith and Order Advisory Group which exists to give theological support to the Church's ecumenical activity. However, such ecumenical involvement notwithstanding, in this essay Packer dissents from the prevailing ecumenical approach.

He argues instead for a return to what he believes to be the classic Reformation position, put forward, for example, in Article XIX, that the Church is the invisible fellowship of all those who believe in the gospel, and is outwardly identified by the proclamation of the gospel in word and sacrament.

> The Church is essentially a fellowship of believers, the totality of those whom Christ has united to himself through the Holy Spirit. What constitutes the Church is not any of its historical outward features – papacy, hierarchy, succession, or any institutional means of grace – but the actual grace-given reality of faith in the Christ of the Gospel. Faith is primary, because Christ, and the Holy Spirit, and the forgiveness of sins, are primary. But since these primary realities are not in any sense visible to human eyes, the Church which they bring into being cannot be visible either. As Luther insisted, the Holy Catholic Church of the Creeds is an object, not of sight, but of faith . . .

> Where the Gospel is, faith is, and where faith is, there the Church is, whatever institutions may be lacking; but no group or organization can be acknowledged as the Church while it lacks the Gospel. The Church becomes visible and identifiable, not by flaunting some historical pedigree of ministerial succession, but by professing and proclaiming the apostolic gospel by word and sacrament.[13]

Because he takes this view of the nature of the Church, Packer is critical of current Church of England ecumenical policy for giving priority to issues of ministerial order over issues of evangelical faith:

> It is commonly said that Anglican unity is 'cultic' rather than 'confessional' and that the Anglican Communion is not a 'confessional' body. It is assumed that this is to its credit; but the truth is the reverse. Basic to the biblical ideas of the Church, as we saw, is the thought of acknowledging and maintaining the 'one faith'. Every church, therefore, should be a 'confessional' body. Our historic formularies show that this was our Reformers' ideal for the Church of England. Unhappily, in recent years the Church has appeared to be more concerned about episcopal order than about evangelical faith, and in interchurch negotiations it has been the former rather than the latter which she has stressed as the necessary basis of unity. It is good, no doubt, that she should be in full communion with the Old Catholics, who have the historic episcopate, even though their faith is yet far from evangelical; but it is deplorable that we should not yet have entered into comparable relations with,

for instance, the Church of Scotland. It is hard to say which feature of the 1963 Methodist conversations report was the more regrettable, its calculated laxity in handling the authority of Scripture or its assiduity in writing the whole substance of episcopal ordination for Methodist clergy into the service of reconciliation.

The times, of which these things are signs, call us to right the balance by recovering the historic Anglican awareness that the true and sufficient basis of the unity which closer church relations are to manifest lies not in the realm of ministerial order, but of catholic – that is evangelical – faith.[14]

3. the importance of the episcopate

For traditional Anglo-Catholics the episcopate is critically important because in their view the historical continuity of the episcopal order, an order which is a continuation of the Apostolate instituted by Christ himself, symbolizes and maintains the Church's unity across space and time. A clear example of this understanding of the significance of the episcopate is given, for instance, by the distinguished Anglo-Catholic theologian E. L. Mascall, who writes as follows in his book *Corpus Christi*, in a chapter entitled 'The One Church':

> the Church is not only a mystical organism, the Body and Bride of Christ, *ecclesia de trinitate* and *de Christo*. It is also a community of men and women living within the historical order, the city and army of the living God, *sponsa Christi quae per orbem militat ecclesia*, marked out indeed from other human societies by its supernatural endowments and its concern for man's eternal end, but none the less visible, tangible, and entangled with all the relativities of history. It would therefore be surprising if there were no visible organ by which the church's unity is expressed and maintained, although that unity is not a merely moral, political or organisational unity but an inner and sacramental one. Such an organ is, I would suggest, to be found in the Apostolate, instituted by Christ in the Twelve and expanded through the centuries into the universal Episcopate.[15]

Further on in the same chapter, Mascall reiterates and expands the same point when he writes that:

> as a visible reality in the historic order the Church's unity is established in our Lord's institution of the Apostolate, which

is continued in the universal Episcopate; the bishop is the link between the local and the universal Church. This fact is reflected in the ancient requirement that for the consecration of a new bishop at least three bishops are normally required as consecrators, that is to say, although the diocese gathered around its bishop is the self-coherent local manifestation of the Church, its perpetuation requires, at least in principle and ideally, a repeated recourse to the universal Apostolate.[16]

Because they take this view of the significance of the episcopate, traditional Anglo-Catholics have been happy with the official Anglican line that the historic episcopate is a *sine qua non* for a reunited Church. However, they have been less happy with the recognition of the ministries of non-episcopal Churches lest such recognition should lead to a devaluing of the importance of the episcopate in Anglican theology and practice.

Liberal churchmen with a Catholic outlook, such as Macquarrie for example, have put forward a similar view of the significance of the episcopate to Mascall. In his discussion of the notes of the Church in *Principles of Christian Theology* Macquarrie argues, for instance, that the episcopate is of apostolic origin and helps to ensure the continuing apostolicity of the Church down the generations:

> As with the other notes of the Church, the note of apostolicity has its own embodiment or institutional form to protect it. This form is the episcopate. This office, publicly transmitted by the apostles to their successors and then on through the generations, is the overt, institutional vehicle for ensuring the continuity of that heritage of faith and practice which was likewise transmitted by the apostles.

In addition, Liberal churchmen of a more Protestant outlook have also been prepared to accept that episcopacy is necessary for a reunited Church, not because of a belief that episcopacy is of apostolic origin, but because of a pragmatic conviction that down the centuries it has proved invaluable as a sign and instrument of the Church's unity. For example, in his Bampton lectures Headlam, who was of central churchmanship, declares:

> The Church, entrusted with the sacred gift of the Sacraments, and starting with the rules and customs of the Apostles, gradually laid down its rule of Orders. This rule was in a particular way directed to the promotion of unity. It was with that purpose that the Eucharist was made dependent on the bishop, that the offering of gifts was the liturgical function of

the regular ministry. It was with that purpose that the rules of episcopal ordination were accepted and made universal. A bishop was the officer, not merely of the local church, but of the Catholic Church. Therefore the Church, as a whole, must take part in his consecration, and to secure this the rule grew up that not fewer than three bishops of other churches must be present and take part in the ceremony. This rule was successful. The unity of the Church was preserved by a strong system of order. The local church was made conspicuously a part of the whole Catholic Church, and each generation was solemnly, by the visible sign of succession, connected with past generations. As an external sign of the unity and continuity of the Church, the fact of Apostolic Succession has been of supreme value.[17]

While Evangelicals have been happy to live with episcopacy as a domestic requirement of the Church of England, many Evangelicals have not been willing to accept the place given to bishops in Catholic theology and mainstream Anglican ecumenical thinking. Three examples will demonstrate this point.

Firstly, in his book *Christian Unity* which was published by the IVF in 1945, G. T. Manley, who was a leading Anglican Evangelical in the period before and after World War II, argues that it is impossible to define the particular role and importance of the episcopal office in a way that distinguishes from other forms of church government:

That a historic succession of office and appointment goes back to the second century and probably to the first is a matter of fact; but since in that first century bishops and presbyters were the same persons, we are left still asking what is that material consideration which differentiates the one from the other? St. Jerome in his day protested against the exclusive claims of the bishops, asserting that in Scripture 'bishop and presbyter are one, the latter being a title of age, the former of office,' and even Bishop Bonner in 1543 made the striking admission that it was of 'no importance whether at first the priest made the bishop or the bishop the priest, as in the beginning of the church there was no (or it was very small) difference between a bishop and a priest.'

No doubt there will always be those who prefer the episcopal system on account of the value they attach to historical continuity, and others who think the presbyterian more scriptural and primitive. But surely Bishop Bonner is right in saying that a distinction which is so devoid of foundation, and so subtle as to elude the grasp of the ordinary mind is of 'no importance.'

Can it be wondered at therefore that Christians in India and
China regard the difference between the episcopal and
presbyterian methods of government as something entirely
irrelevant, and as affording no justification for disunion in the
Church?[18]

Because he failed to see any real distinction between episcopal and
non-episcopal forms of church government, Manley was enthusiastic
about the unity scheme adopted by the Church of South India
which, while it adopted an episcopal polity, gave equal status to
those ministers who were episcopally ordained and those who were
not, and rejected any idea of re-ordination for those who lacked
episcopal ordination.

Secondly, a similar impatience about the claims made for
episcopacy is to be found in Michael Green's book *Freed to Serve*
in which he explores the nature of Christian ministry from an
Evangelical point of view:

All Anglicans are committed to the value of episcopacy as a
practical requirement in our Church, we are not committed to
any theory about it, least of all to the view that it represents in
our day of the authority of the apostles. For decades the Church
of South India, though fully episcopal, was not granted
intercommunion by the Church of England upon the insistence
of Anglo-Catholics. It was second-class citizen in the episcopal
club because some of its clergy had not been episcopally
ordained. The future in reunion lies not with imparting episcopal
ordination, reordination or conditional reordination to non-
episcopal ministries, but the coming together, perhaps by
solemn covenanting, of Churches whose members and ministers
accept one another as Christ has accepted them. There is little
doubt that episcopacy has a great deal to offer, as a symbol of
unity and catholicity on the one hand, and as a pastoral office
on the other. But it will not be accepted, nor should it be if it
comes with the implicit or explicit rider that no other ministries
are valid in the church of God.[19]

Thirdly, Melvin Tinker argues, in a book which he edited with the
rather lurid title *The Anglican Evangelical Crisis*, that according to
traditional Anglican teaching episcopacy is unnecessary for either
the being or the wellbeing of the Church. He argues that in the
New Testament we can find no trace of the idea that apostolic
authorization was required for the existence of churches and their
ministries (he cites the churches in Rome and Antioch as counter
examples), or that there is any kind of apostolic succession other

than the succession of the apostolic doctrine, and that: 'according to Article 6, we are required only to believe those things demonstrable from Scripture'.[20]

Furthermore, he says:

> As we saw in Article 19, succession is not offered as one of the marks of the church. Richard Hooker, although he prized episcopacy, did not consider it necessary and said that 'The church hath power by universal consent to take it away.' But not only, in accordance with traditional Anglican teaching, is episcopacy not of the esse (essence-being) of the church, neither is it absolutely necessary for its bene esse (well being) – we are merely told that it is something which has been received from ancient times and is continuing; it is something which is not contrary to Scripture. So far as traditional historic Anglicanism is concerned, episcopacy is a matter of indifference. We should, therefore, not be enticed into accepting a view of episcopacy which is scripturally and theologically deficient. We are not to allow this innovative doctrine to hinder fellowship and work with fellow believers who have a different ministerial structure, so that they cannot enter our pulpits or celebrate around the Lord's table – that is a scandal and must be overcome.[21]

It might be tempting to think that the attitudes to unity and episcopacy which I have just illustrated are the opinions of a few Evangelical extremists. On the contrary, however, they are in fact typical of thinking among Evangelicals in general, even among those of a moderate persuasion.

Thus the NEAC conference of 1967, which is widely regarded as the point at which the Evangelical party came out of its ghetto and embraced the structures of the Church of England, refused to acknowledge the theological necessity of episcopacy:

> We maintain that matters of faith take priority over matters of order. Our basic loyalty is to the Word of God. While we accept that in England episcopacy seems the only pattern for reunion, we do not believe that it is a theological necessity. We affirm that regional Churches should be free to develop their own life, culture and forms of government.[22]

The late David Watson, who was passionate about the need for the unity of God's people and worked hard for the reconciliation of the Catholics and Protestants in Northern Ireland, nevertheless declares in his book *I Believe in the Church* that:

Christ's Church is not to be seen as a vast totalitarian, monolithic structure, based on the principle of organisational, structural and liturgical uniformity. Christian unity, envisaged by the New Testament, is surely something quite different.[23]

He argues, therefore, that there should be mutual recognition of a variety of different forms of ministry:

we need to recognise the God-given ministries that undoubtedly do exist in the various strands of the Christian church. Whether or not there has been episcopal ordination, we should accept those in whom there is the charisma of leadership, service and teaching. If the first apostles had the generosity and wisdom to accept Paul's mission and ministry to the Gentiles on the grounds that God was manifestly with him, who are we to reject the ministries of others who are not of our communion?[24]

And even George Carey, writing in his book *The Meeting of the Waters*, published in 1985 when he was Principal of Trinity College, Bristol, stresses the essentially spiritual unity of the Church, the fact that unity does not mean ecclesiastical uniformity, and that monoepiscopacy should not be seen as a theological necessity:

While we must not undervalue the importance of membership in the visible church, we must recognise that membership in the body of Christ is constituted not by the external marks of joining the church, but by spiritual birth . . . This spiritual unity should dominate and colour our whole theology of the church. Have as high a doctrine of the organic unity of the church as you like, so long as your doctrine of spiritual birth is higher. We are all one in Christ Jesus. We cannot classify Christians by human organisations; we dare not say definitely that all Catholics are Christians or that all Baptists or all Methodists are Christians, or that unbaptised people cannot be Christians. Our ecclesiastical rules cannot confine God's Spirit – the Spirit leaps over human barriers.[25]

One thing we must remind ourselves. Unity is not uniformity. The existence of separate Christian groups in one area is not in itself incompatible with unity, any more than the house churches of the New Testament represented a division of the total Christian body in one place. Many of our denominational churches reflect different temperamental or sociological leanings and so enrich the body of Christ by the variety they express. A dull uniformity is not the quest of unity. Rather, what divides Christians is a refusal to accept one another in Christ, and this is tragically mirrored in denominational bans which forbid our meeting around the table of the Lord.[26]

There may be good reasons for embracing monoepiscopacy, for example, but I find no cogent reason for saying it is of the essence of Christianity. I might well consider it desirable as a form of church order, and it may be an element that would lead me to choose this Christian community rather than that one, but to make monoepiscopacy binding on all Christians as a dogma to accept would be to place on them a burden which the New Testament does not make.[27]

4. differing proposals for reunion

At the moment the official policy of the Church of England with regard to reunion consists of pursuing bilateral and multilateral agreements at a denominational level with partner Churches at home and overseas with the intention, in England at least, that the eventual outcome of all these separate agreements will be a single, united, episcopally led, national Church. However, this present policy is only one of a number of different schemes for achieving a reunited Church put forward by Anglican theologians since the 1930s. The following examples will illustrate this point.

In 1938 a joint conference of representatives of the Church of England and the Free Church Federal Council chaired by the Archbishop of Canterbury, Cosmo Lang, produced an Outline of a Reunion Scheme for the Church of England and the Free Churches in England. This scheme suggested that all the Churches involved should come together in one united episcopal Church on the basis set out in the Lambeth Quadrilateral with the orders of existing Free Church Ministers being recognized in the new Church without any form of re-ordination or fresh commissioning. The 1938 proposals came to nothing, and in 1946 the then Archbishop of Canterbury, Geoffrey Fisher, called in a sermon in Cambridge for a different approach in which the various different Free Churches would each individually consider how they might enter into full fellowship and communion with the Church of England.[28]

Building on this idea, G. K. A. Bell suggested in his book *Christian Unity*, mentioned at the beginning of this chapter, that reunion should consist in the establishment of a fellowship of episcopal Churches in communion with each other:

All Churches maintaining the Holy Scriptures, the Creeds and the two Dominical Sacraments, and possessing the Historic Episcopate, while in each case preserving their local tradition, worship and discipline, would be in communion with one another. They would also express their union through a common organ, as the Churches of the Anglican Communion express theirs through the Lambeth Conference. The Councils of Bishops would again become, as they were in antiquity, the permanent 'organ by which the unity of distant Churches could find expression without any derogation from their rightful autonomy'. There would still be denominational conferences such as those of the Anglican Bishops at Lambeth. There would also be territorial conferences of the bishops of the Churches in communion with one another in the same region. Above all there would be the Oecumenical conferences of bishops representing all the Churches united in the acceptance of one another's episcopal orders.[29]

The English Free Churches could enter into this fellowship simply by receiving bishops from any Church possessing the historic episcopate. Because their ministers are 'already ordained as ministers in the Church of God' there would be no question of these ministers requiring episcopal re-ordination.[30]

The Anglican–Methodist Unity scheme of the 1960s proposed moving towards a united Anglican Methodist Church by a formal union of the two Churches following a period of full communion and interchangeability of ministry between them. In their book *Growing into Union* a joint team of Anglo-Catholic and Evangelical writers opposed to the Anglican–Methodist scheme produced another possible pattern for unity. They suggest a 'one stage scheme' in which they look for:

a united Church to grow up between the existing denominations by accessions from existing congregations spread slowly over the years. The united Church would start as one or two isolated parish-type areas, grow into an archipelago, and eventually approach a solid shape in region after region, until the participating denominations finally disappeared and a new English Church had replaced them. In every case the transfer would occur only when the local Christians were agreed in desiring it, and although the parent denomination and the united Church authorities would be involved in negotiating, the local church or churches would be granted full powers to take the decision for themselves.[31]

John Wenham was an Evangelical scholar of an independent outlook, and his book *The Renewal and Unity of the Church in England* was his personal response to the call issued by the British Council of Churches in 1964 for Christians to work and pray for unity between the Churches by Easter 1980. In this book he calls for the establishment of a 'broadly based commission from all denominations' which would produce reports on the theological and structural prerequisites for a united Church. These reports would then be considered by local study groups. Suggesting a three-year programme of study between 1973 and 1976, Wenham argues that:

> In 1976–7 the findings could be brought up successively to district conferences (not later than December), to regional conferences (not later than the Easter holiday) and to a national conference in September. We might find that we had the will, the pattern, and the overwhelming national support to form a united Church by Easter 1980. Since much of the preparatory spade-work would have already been done during the years of study, it is conceivable that three years of intensive work might be enough to see a united Church consummated.[32]

We have already seen Stibbs arguing that unity ought to be pursued at a local level and Tinker returns to this theme in 1996 in *The Anglican Evangelical Crisis*:

> It is theoretically possible to have a 'unity' of denominations or only have one 'superstructure', and yet be far removed from the unity of which the New Testament speaks – unity in Christ and in truth. This is not to say that where possible one should not seek a greater understanding between such organizations, and where appropriate a sharing of resources – but is this really Biblical ecumenism? Would it not be more in line with the New Testament view of the Church to seek closer fellowship, a recognition of ministries, a coming together between local churches which do confess and have that oneness in Christ and in truth? That is what would commonly be called evangelical ecumenism. Should not this be the prayer of evangelical believers, as it was of the great Richard Baxter?[33]

5. the place of the Papacy in a united Church

At the Reformation the Church of England took a strongly anti-papal stance, a stance most clearly reflected in the prayer in Cranmer's litany: 'From the bishop of Rome and all his detestable enormities, good Lord deliver us.'

However, from the end of the sixteenth century onwards there has been an ambivalence in Church of England attitudes towards the Papacy, with widespread hostility to the theology and exercise of papal authority being balanced, in some writers at least, by the belief that a reformed Papacy ought to have that degree of primacy that was granted to it by the Church of the early centuries.

This ambivalence still continues. Following Vatican II and the development of closer ecumenical relationships between Anglicans and Roman Catholics which followed from it through the work of ARCIC and other instruments of ecumenical contact and cooperation, there has been a growing feeling in ecumenical circles in the Church of England that Anglicans should be willing to accept some form of papal oversight. However, there are also continuing doubts about the claims made for the authority of the Pope in Roman Catholic theology.

The House of Bishops' response to the papal encyclical on ecumenism *Ut Unum Sint* clearly reflects these two aspects of ecumenical thinking about the Papacy.

On the one hand, the bishops suggest that Anglicans can see a need for a universal primacy:

> Anglicans and Roman Catholics are at one in their understanding of the episcopate as a ministry involving not only oversight of each local church but also a care for the universal communion of which each church is a member. ARCIC I sees the office of the universal primate as a special and particular case of this care for universal communion which is proper for the episcopal office itself. Anglicans are thus by no means opposed to the principle and practice of a personal ministry at the world level in the service of unity. Indeed, increasingly their experience of the Anglican Communion is leading them to appreciate the proper need, alongside communal and collegial ministries, for a personal service of unity in the faith.[34]

They also argue that this ministry of unity must 'have doctrinal and disciplinary elements'.[35] On the other hand they also suggest that the doctrine of papal infallibility is one that requires further discussion and note that:

> In matters of discipline and the oversight of the communion of the Church we should not minimize the serious obstacles that still exist because of the present Roman Catholic understanding of the jurisdiction attributed to the primacy of the Bishop of Rome. The claim that the Bishop of Rome has by divine

institution ordinary, immediate and universal jurisdiction over the whole Church is seen by some as a threat to the integrity of the episcopal college and to the apostolic authority of the bishops, those brothers Peter was commanded to strengthen.[36]

This ' yes . . . but' attitude to the Papacy does not go far enough for some on the Anglo-Catholic wing of the Church of England who are already prepared to accept the authority of the Pope (while not accepting the papal condemnation of Anglican orders in 1896). By contrast there are also those on the Evangelical side of the Church who think that the Church of England should simply stick by the Reformation rejection of the Papacy.

Thus Richard Bewes, writing on behalf of the Church of England Evangelical Council in response to the recent ARCIC report *The Gift of Authority*, points back to what Cranmer and Calvin had to say on the matter:

> The great Thomas Cranmer on the very day of his martyrdom specifically rejected the authority of the Pope as being incompatible with the authority of Christ. His rejection of papal claims was consistent with the way in which all the Reformers recognised the deep problems of the Roman Catholic account of authority. It is well worth recalling that in Calvin's *Institutes* Bk IV, chapter 6, section 1, when he discusses the question of authority in the Roman Church as the fundamental problem: 'The capstone of the whole structure, that is, the primacy of the Roman See, from which they strive to prove that the Church catholic is their exclusive possession . . . They try to persuade the world that the chief and almost sole bond of Church unity is that we cleave to the Roman See.'

> It is amazing that in 450 years we are not offered anything more substantial to bring about visible unity. If the Roman Catholic Church is really unwilling to re-examine the teaching of the Word of God on ecclesial authority, then the whole ecumenical process has not come very far at all.[37]

6. conclusion

The material that I have brought forward in this chapter suggests three things.

First, in developing its ecumenical policy, the Church of England needs to take its internal theological diversity more seriously than it has done in the past. There needs to be a recognition that there is a significant constituency within the Church of England that remains unconvinced by the Church's official approach to ecumenism because it is rooted in an understanding of the Church that it does not accept.

Second, there is a need to listen to radical, feminist, missiological and local voices. Their absence from this survey indicates their absence from the Church of England's conversation about ecumenism and this is something that needs to be rectified.

Third, the material we have looked at indicates that there is a need to ask basic questions about the nature of ecumenism, such as the following:

- What are the proper sources of ecumenical thinking and how should we use the Bible and tradition in a responsible manner?
- What is the goal of the ecumenical process?
- Should ecumenism operate locally, nationally, or globally or on all levels at once?
- Are there any theological givens with which we have to work or are we free to build a united Church as we see fit?
- How do we ensure that ecumenism remains properly related to mission?

All these issues are pursued in the contributions to this book. This chapter has argued that they should be considered against the backcloth of the internal diversity of the Church of England and that Conservative Evangelical views of the Church and its unity should be taken more seriously.

chapter four

the use of the Bible in ecumenical dialogue involving Anglicans

Joy Tetley

part I: setting the scene: context and subtext

Those who produced the King James Version of the Bible described the Scriptures as 'a treasury of most costly jewels'. Three questions arise: Who holds the key to that treasury? Beautiful as they are, does it contain but a jumble of jewels? Wherein lies their costliness?

It is important to begin this exploration by indicating something of my own context and perspective on this issue. No position is neutral. The Scriptures excite me and have done for many years, from childhood through to a life of study and ministry. That is the setting for what follows.

The Scriptures point to a many-splendoured and multi-faceted vision; one that stretches human horizons. They disclose a tantalizing God, a God who will not be tamed or confined, a God who breaks out of boundaries, even sacred boundaries, a God who constantly surprises and challenges, yet is utterly trustworthy and faithful, a God whose burning holiness paradoxically leads to divine engagement with what is far less than holy, a God whose passionate love prompts both devotion and savage abuse, a God bursting with creativity, vitality and joy, who nonetheless weeps with those who weep, a God who is greater than all that is, yet with a personal touch that is awesome in its intensity. This God yearns for communion with humankind, calling forth a responsive longing.

The Scriptures which present us with this God were born out of experience; out of faith and doubt; out of celebration and struggle; out of joy and anguish. In many and various ways, they seek to articulate the felt impact of the inbreaking (or, indeed, perceived withdrawal) of God. They are not works of systematic theology. They *are* full of theological reflection, but hardly ever in the abstract.

They are prompted by particular, often compelling, situations and coloured in their expression by their culture, religious background and context. But they are nonetheless recognizable. All human life is there. And all human life in all shades of relationship with a God who both comforts and confronts. In these ancient documents from a faraway world, we can still come face to face with ourselves and with the living God.

Both the Church and the world are today full of questions: curious questions, searching questions, sharp questions, heart-breaking questions, inarticulate questions. So are the Scriptures. Here is an area with enormous potential for creative interaction. Too often the Bible is thought of as a neatly tied-up package of propositions, a rule book containing human interest stories to help us swallow the medicine. That is a travesty. When we allow the Scriptures to be seized by the unpredictable Spirit of truth, they are anything but cut and dried. Like the God to be met in them, they are living and active – and they refuse to be domesticated.

Through the richly varied expressions of Scripture there is a dialogue going on: a dialogue between God and humanity and creation, creation, humanity and God; a dialogue characterized by passion on both sides. Strong feelings abound, whether of joy and delight or of hurt and anger. The conversation is rarely a superficial one, though it can be very mundane in form. Sometimes it is far from polite. Yet of such tempestuous exchange is rich relationship born. And the Scriptures are fundamentally about relationship, even when treating of law, as Psalm 119 so eloquently testifies.

The dialogue goes on. It must go on if there is to be any hope of deepening understanding. The Bible can still be a powerful facilitator of its development. It provides a wealth of basic indicators which need very little cultural translation. Questions are near to the heart of the matter. In the witness of the Scriptures, questions play a key role in the divine–human dialogue. They are much in evidence from beginning to end. It has been calculated, for example, that in John's Gospel alone there are well over a hundred of them. Significantly, there are not nearly as many direct answers! The first question ascribed to God in the Scriptures is asked of primal humankind in the story of Adam and Eve's fall. It is, to say the least, a penetrating one: 'Where are you?' (Genesis 3.9). That challenge has not lost its relevance. It invites honest response, even when we would rather hide ourselves from the presence of God. Such a response may well involve discomfiture. But, as Adam and Eve discovered, it opens the way for ongoing relationship with the God who continues to make caring provision, even when things have gone badly wrong. The delightful picture of God making clothes for the exposed human couple says it all (Genesis 3.21). By that stage, God has prompted them to articulate and own their condition by a series of targeted questions. When that is done, their situation can be effectively addressed. It is a telling narrative.

The paradigm of Eden sets the tone. The God of the Bible is a questioning, searching God. God's most important question of all comes in the form of Jesus. As an ordinand once put it, Jesus is an arresting combination of question mark and exclamation mark. In Jesus, God exclaims both in joy and in pain, both in tenderness and in anger, 'I love you.' In Jesus, God asks, without any coercion, 'Can you love me?' In their various ways, all of the Gospel traditions confront us with that searching invitation. And all of the Gospel traditions present Jesus as posing not a few questions. From the records we have, it seems clear that Jesus made people think, that he was economical with straight answers, that he made people confused and angry, that he aroused hatred and conspiracy as well as wonder and devotion. 'Who then is this?' That question remains with us.

The questioning God, incarnate in Jesus, does, it seems, respect our freedom. We can ignore the questions. Or, like the scriptural people of God, we can hazard a whole variety of answers. Like our forebears, too, we have the freedom to cast our questions in the direction of God. The Bible leaves us in no doubt that it is a two-way process. In fact, a strong thread in the biblical witness seems to suggest that human beings are positively encouraged to question God. It is an important part of deepening relationship. So, in the text of Job as we now have it, though the afflicted one might eventually be reduced to silence by the One Eric Heaton describes as divine head teacher, that same authority rebukes Eliphaz at the end with the words, 'My wrath is kindled against you and your two friends, for you have not spoken of me what is right, as my servant Job has' (42.7). And unlike his pious friends, Job has spoken of God things very daring in the context of his time.

According to Scripture, honesty really is the best policy. That is powerfully demonstrated in the cry of desolation from the cross, as recorded in Mark's Gospel: 'My God, my God, why hast thou forsaken me?' 'My God, my God, why?' Why? There is the quintessential question of our human existence. It is humanity's deepest hope that, somehow, God feels the full force of that question; that God does indeed know what it is like to feel God-forsaken. And out of that great, unanswered question, shouted into the darkness, comes a new beginning, comes not an answer but a response, comes a way through that breaks the bounds of possibility. And there, quite literally, is the crux of the matter. The God we encounter in the Bible is, at heart, the God of cross and resurrection: the God who comes to us where we are and goes to hell and back with us and for us. To this God we can respond; to this God we can, if we choose, entrust our lives; with this God we can participate in the adventure of redemption; with this God we can reach out in love to the world. But this God we can never fully explain. God is who God is. Woe betide us if we try to confine this God to our own agenda.

The biblical presentation of God is kaleidoscopic rather than definitive. The more we look, the more the patterns change. That leaves us in our proper place: wondering; grappling with poetry, mystery, questions and paradox rather than presuming to control the great enigma who is God. The God of the Scriptures will not be pinned down – except, briefly, on a cross. But the cross cannot hold him. As St John puts it, 'in the place where he was crucified there was a garden' (John 19.41). The place of stark horror becomes the place of new life and fruitfulness. Out of the darkness and suffering is born a new beginning. This Easter garden, grown out of evil and anguish, is far more fertile than primal Eden. Here love triumphs over hate, forgiveness breaks through the negative spiral of vengeance, joy emerges through pain, life conquers death – not in wishful thinking, but in God's reality. Here, indeed, is the 'truth' that Pilate asked for – the truth of sacrificial divine love, beyond all telling – and *true* for every age and generation.

And that leaves us, in the end, facing another thoroughly biblical question: 'Do you believe this?' (John 11.26).

part II: surveying the material

We now turn to survey the use of the Bible in ecumenical dialogue involving Anglicans, adopting that interrogative approach which is so characteristic of the Scriptures themselves. How do such dialogues view the significance of Scripture? What approaches do they take towards the interpretation of Scripture? What might be the issues raised by the methodologies adopted? It is important, therefore, to state that this is not a paper treating of biblical hermeneutics *per se*. The specific focus is the way in which ecumenical engagement deals with the Bible and it is offered as a discussion starter in this regard.

A perspectives on the significance of Scripture

In all ecumenical dialogues, the canonical Scriptures[1] are held to be of the utmost significance. The ways in which that significance is expressed display both commonalities and interesting variations and shades of emphasis. In most cases, the crucial role of Scripture is almost a 'given'. There is thus little teasing out and examination of the phraseology used to convey its essential and honoured place. So, words like 'normative' and 'authoritative' are allowed to stand proud. The precise sense and implications of such words tend to be neither defined nor explored. Were they to be, ecumenical conversation might find itself in a fascinating, challenging and potentially very fruitful area. It might even open up fresh perspectives on long-term issues of debate such as matters to do with ministry. It would also, of course, be characterized by risk; not least because approaches to the Bible, both historically and now, have a propensity to arouse great passions. Over the significance of these core texts, lives have been given and taken. They (both texts and lives) matter. All the more reason, perhaps, not to gloss over the questions these texts raise.

Having said this, it should be noted that Anglican–Roman Catholic dialogue does make some moves in the direction of a journey of exploration. Awareness is displayed that here is an issue to be addressed. Indeed, responses to the publication of ARCIC's first statement on *Authority* (1976) brought home the fact that concerns about the primacy of Scripture were still very much alive – to such an extent that the matter needed to be highlighted in the Elucidation produced by the Commission, and included in *The Final Report*:[2]

> Our documents have been criticized for failing to give an adequate account of the primary authority of Scripture in the Church . . . Our description of 'the inspired documents . . . as a normative record of the authentic foundation of the faith' (para 2) has been felt to be an inadequate statement of the truth.[3]

Proceeding by way of response and elucidation (an interesting methodology in itself) ARCIC clarified thus:

> The basis of our approach to Scripture is the affirmation that Christ is God's final word to man – his eternal Word made flesh . . . The person and work of Jesus Christ, preached by the apostles and set forth and interpreted in the New Testament writings, through the inspiration of the Holy Spirit, are the primary norm for Christian faith and life . . .

No endeavour of the Church to express the truth can add to the revelation already given. Moreover, since the Scriptures are the uniquely inspired witness to divine revelation, the Church's expression of that revelation must be tested by its consonance with Scripture.[4]

Inevitably, as well as clarifying matters, the 'Elucidation' highlighted the need to pursue some questions further. The Faith and Order Group of the Church of England (FOAG) pointed clearly to this in its response to the ARCIC *Final Report*:

Accordingly, while ARCIC plainly gives primacy to the authority of Scripture, the Commission has not argued for Scripture being the sole and exclusive source of guidance . . . Although the Commission can hardly be held guilty, as they have been accused, of failing to give account of the primacy of Scripture, there still lie behind their reports questions about the authority and interpretation of Scripture, about the significance of the closing of the Canon, and about the dynamic nature of tradition. *These are questions which in the future Anglicans and Roman Catholics will need to explore together.*[5] (italics mine)

In terms of methodology, it is salient to note here that the process of 'interested parties' (e.g. denominational faith and order bodies) responding critically (in its best sense) to either the finished work of dialogues, or to work in progress, can be a most constructive dimension of the work's wider reception in the Churches involved.

The Gift of Authority (ARCIC's third agreed statement on authority)[6] takes on and develops somewhat the ongoing discussion concerning the significance of Scripture. The statement itself stresses that it is intended to 'prompt further theological reflection'.[7] Its very publication is so that it may be widely discussed and carefully evaluated.[8] In relation to all the issues raised, the place of Scripture included, the matter is most certainly not considered closed. As the Statement's Introduction (paragraph 3) puts it:

the authorities of our two communions have asked for further exploration of areas where, although there has been convergence, they believe that a necessary consensus has not yet been achieved. These areas include . . . the relationship between Scripture, Tradition and the exercise of teaching authority . . .

The Gift of Authority again uses words such as 'unique', 'inspired', 'normative' and 'witness' to underline the importance of Scripture. To these is added another, which in the *Final Report* had not been so specifically employed: 'authoritative'. So we read that the Church 'regards this corpus alone as the inspired Word of God written and, as such, uniquely authoritative'.[9] It seems, therefore, that the high status of Scripture has been further emphasized. Nonetheless, much depends on how all these summary words are to be understood – particularly in relation to what are regarded as other sources of authority, notably 'the Church' and 'Tradition'. We shall return to these matters below.

In relation to the significance of Scripture, the ARCIC documents effectively begin to identify an agenda. Though their intention might be to clarify and resolve the issues, what they say (and what they do not say) indicates the need for further exploratory work. As part of the wide discussion called for by *The Gift of Authority*, for example, it is vital that the implications of the phrase 'uniquely authoritative' are thoroughly unravelled. Wherein lies the authority of this 'uniquely authoritative' gift? And in what sense is that authority unique?

When we turn to examples from Anglican dialogues with Protestant Churches, we find similar terminology being used in relation to Scripture, but without so much of the questioning edge found in the ARCIC documents. To a considerable extent, agreement between the interlocutors is virtually assumed. The *Anglican–Lutheran International Commission Report* (Pullach, 1972) puts it thus:

> 17 The Anglican and Lutheran Churches hold that it is Jesus Christ, God and Man, born, crucified, risen, and ascended for the salvation of mankind, in whom all Scriptures find their focus and fulfilment. They are at one in accepting the Holy Scriptures of the Old and New Testaments as the sufficient, inspired, and authoritative record and witness, prophetic and apostolic, to God's revelation in Jesus Christ.

> 18 Both Churches hold that through the proclamation of the Gospel and administration of the sacraments, based on the same Scriptures and empowered by the Holy Spirit, Christ is speaking to us and is active amongst us today, calling us to live and serve in his name.

> 19 Both Churches hold that nothing should be preached, taught, or ordered in the Church which contradicts the Word of God as it is proclaimed in Scripture.

The Report of the Anglican–Reformed International Commission, 1984, *God's Reign and Our Unity*, does not feel it necessary to spell things out quite so directly. The Scriptures are described as 'the authoritative standard of faith' (paragraph 40), and the two Testaments are described in terms of their witness to God's sheer grace and faithfulness (paragraph 26). The primacy of Scripture permeates the whole document but it is nowhere explicitly defined.

In the Meissen Agreement of 1988, we find the perception of Scripture as 'gift', that which is common to all participating Churches as a dimension of the communion they already share. This gift (by implication from God) is 'the authentic record of God's revelation in Jesus Christ and . . . the norm for Christian faith and life' (paragraph 9). The first point of agreement in faith noted by the dialogue in the list contained in paragraph 15 is:

> We accept the authority of the canonical Scriptures of the Old and New Testaments. We read the Scriptures liturgically in the course of the Church's year.

Similarly, the Porvoo Common Statement (1992), *Together in Mission and Ministry*, resulting from Conversations between the British and Irish Anglican Churches and the Nordic and Baltic Lutheran Churches, begins its summary list of 'What we agree in faith' with a statement about the Bible:

> We accept the *canonical scriptures* of the Old and New Testaments to be sufficient, inspired and authoritative record and witness, prophetic and apostolic, to God's revelation in Jesus Christ. We read the Scriptures as part of public worship in the language of the people, believing that in the Scriptures – as the Word of God and testifying to the gospel – eternal life is offered to all humanity, and that they contain everything necessary to salvation.

This is clearly a fuller affirmation than that of Meissen, drawing on Pullach (see above) as well as adding its own gloss (including, for example, an allusion to Article VI of the Thirty-Nine Articles). There is much in this fascinating paragraph that could be further teased out and explored, but readers are left to do this for themselves. Why, for example, is the phrase 'canonical scriptures' italicized? What, then, is to be made of those other books (included as an integral part of Roman Catholic editions of the Bible) which did not come to be agreed as canonical by the early Church but which, as Article VI puts it, 'the Church doth read for example of life and instruction of manners'? How are we to understand each of the catalogue of adjectives contained in the first sentence of the paragraph? In what sense are the Old and New Testaments 'the Word of God'? How does the Word relate to the Word who became flesh?

The Reuilly Common Statement (1999), *Called to Witness and Service*, resulting from Conversations between the British and Irish Anglican Churches and the French Lutheran and Reformed Churches, contains a compressed version of Porvoo (with reference to Meissen, Pullach and Leuenberg) as its opening item of agreement in faith (paragraph 31a):

> We accept the authority of the canonical Scriptures of the Old and New Testaments. We read the Scriptures liturgically in the course of the Church's year. We believe that through the gospel, God offers eternal life to all humanity, and that the Scriptures contain everything necessary to salvation.

It is apparent from this brief glimpse at some Anglican–Protestant dialogues that

a) there is assured (if somewhat unexplored) agreement on the primacy of scriptural authority;

b) there is a common sense that Scripture is to be Christologically understood and interpreted; and

c) the dialogues employ a methodology which receives, carries forward and sometimes builds on the labours and insights of previous ecumenical Conversations.[10]

B approaches to the interpretation of Scripture

In varying degrees, related perhaps to how much can readily be assumed, all the dialogues ascribe a very high significance to Scripture. When it comes to how Scripture is to be interpreted (and by whom) most agreed statements and reports give little explicit indication of their hermeneutical stance. Indeed, the reader might be forgiven for detecting in many of the dialogues something verging on the 'proof-text syndrome'. Verses and passages are cited which might be thought to support a position being put forward.[11] Only rarely is the original context of a reference taken into account. Using now established ecumenical methodology many citations are simply carried forward unexamined from preceding documents. There is little attention given as to how (and if) the gap might be bridged between 'here' and 'there', 'now' and 'then'. There is also little sign of engagement with the well-populated world of biblical scholarship in all its manifold expressions. It is pertinent to ask why this should be so. Does the high standing of Scripture render it 'untouchable'? Would grappling with biblical interpretation challenge consensus and/or open too many wounds?

The Pullach Report of the Anglican–Lutheran International Commission is one of the few Anglican–Protestant dialogues to touch on these matters. After affirming that the Holy Scriptures are 'the sufficient, inspired and authoritative record and witness, prophetic and apostolic, to God's revelation in Jesus Christ', the Report goes on to say:

> 16 Within both Churches different attitudes exist concerning the nature of inspiration and the ways and means of interpreting the Scriptures, and these attitudes run across the denominational boundaries.

> 9 Both Churches agree in stressing the need and responsibility for a continuing interpretation of the biblical texts in order to communicate the Gospel of salvation to all men in different times and changing circumstances.[12]

The diversity of attitudes 'across the denominational boundaries' perhaps needs more open attention in ecumenical conversations, with regard to other challenging areas, as well as the Bible. Pullach stresses 'the need and responsibility for a continuing interpretation of the biblical texts' as part of the imperative of proclaiming the gospel in this and every generation. The report does not elaborate on how this might be done, but it does go on to indicate that interpretation should have its limits and its particular practitioners:

> [The Scriptures] teach that the whole Church, and especially the ministry of the Church, has received the responsibility for guarding all proclamation and interpretation from error by guiding, admonishing, and judging and by formulating doctrinal statements, the biblical witness always being the final authority and court of appeal.[13]

It is possible, then, for interpretation to be in error, and the Church's ministry has a special responsibility to see that such error is identified and corrected. That which is being interpreted (the Bible) is also the final arbiter of the acceptability or otherwise of any suggested interpretations. Power, indeed, it might seem. Yet, in a very real sense, any reading of any passage in Scripture is always an interpretation of it. In the end, surely, it is only other interpreters of the text who can 'judge' interpretations. And all interpreters work, willy-nilly, out of their own contexts and agendas. The 'plain sense of Scripture' can appear very different when viewed from differing perspectives. Scripture as 'the final authority and court of appeal' requires human mediators. Who are they to be? It is of no little significance, then, who is given authority in these matters and on what criteria they operate (a question already noted in relation to ARCIC's approach).

Such concerns are perhaps of particular pertinence when it comes to Anglican–Roman Catholic dialogue. As we have noted above, ARCIC's first statement on authority prompted the need for an 'Elucidation', not least in the area of Scripture. Both *The Final Report* and the subsequent *Gift of Authority* document also raise questions in the area of interpretation (which area, it should be noted, they deal with more fully than the Anglican–Protestant dialogues).

ARCIC's *Elucidation I* on *Authority*, after stressing that 'the Scriptures are the uniquely inspired witness to divine revelation', goes on to assert that

> the Church's expression of that revelation must be tested by its consonance with Scripture. This does not mean simply repeating the words of Scripture, but also both delving into their deeper significance and unravelling their implications for Christian belief and practice. It is impossible to do this without resorting to current language and thought. Consequently the teaching of the Church will often be expressed in words that are different from the original words of scripture without being alien to their meaning . . . This combination of permanence in the revealed truth and continuous exploration of its meaning is what is meant by Christian tradition.[14]

Elucidation 2 then goes on to outline two different (but not mutually incompatible) ways of viewing 'tradition', as defined above:

> One approach is primarily concerned never to go beyond the bounds of Scripture. Under the guidance of the Holy Spirit undiscovered riches and truths are sought in the Scriptures in order to illuminate the faith according to the needs of each generation . . . Another approach . . . draws upon everything in human experience and thought which will give the content of revelation its fullest expression and widest application. It is primarily concerned with the growth of the seed of God's word from age to age.[15]

Scripture, then, is either quarry or 'seed'. In both cases, there will be a fundamental relationship with the raw material of the texts but the outcome of the interpretation process may well change their shape and appearance.

The Gift of Authority takes matters further. It states that the Scriptures 'bring together diverse streams of Jewish and Christian traditions' which 'reveal the way God's Word has been received, interpreted and passed on in specific contexts, according to the needs, the culture and the circumstances of the people of God'. This is a refreshing acknowledgement of contextuality and inter-textuality within the Scriptures and of an interrelationship between texts which is not always smooth and harmonious. *The Gift of Authority* also reminds us how important it is to recognize and explore the crucial relationship between 'the First Testament' and 'the New Testament'. It interprets that as follows:

> Within the New Testament we can see how the Scriptures of the First Testament were both received as revelation of the one true God and also reinterpreted and re-received as revelation of his final Word in Christ.[16]

This notion of 're-reception' is a significant feature of *The Gift of Authority*'s contribution to (fledgling) ecumenical discussion in the area of biblical hermeneutics. The Church, it asserts, must be

> free to receive the apostolic Tradition in new ways according to the situations by which it is confronted . . . Thus, there may be a rediscovery of elements that were neglected and a fresh remembrance of the promises of God, leading to renewal of the Church's 'Amen'. There may also be a sifting of what has been received because some of the formulations of the Tradition are seen to be inadequate or even misleading in a new context.[17]

In order for such 'sifting' and 're-reception' to happen, the *whole* of the apostolic Tradition must be carefully handed on from generation to generation. What is not relevant in one age may become so in another.[18]

All of this raises acutely the question of who brings about 'rediscovery', 'fresh remembrance' and the interpretation of the same for the present age. On what criteria, too, are judgements to be made? And what is meant in this context by the phrase 'the Church'? What does handing on the *whole* of the apostolic Tradition involve, if some is by implication to be kept, as it were, in storage? Here there remains ample scope for elucidation and dialogue.

The Gift of Authority boldly states: 'The meaning of the revealed Gospel of God is fully understood only within the Church.' It goes on to stress that the Church is a community, not 'an aggregate of individual believers'. Moreover, 'the faith of the community precedes the faith of the individual.' Hence:

> Individualistic interpretation of the Scriptures is not attuned to the reading of the text within the life of the Church and is incompatible with the nature of the authority of the revealed Word of God (cf. 2 Pet. 1.20-21). Word of God and Church of God cannot be put asunder.[19]

This clearly begs a number of questions. Should individuals be so entirely subsumed into the 'community' of the Church that they have no valid contribution to make, unless it lies within the parameters of 'the Church's' definitions? The biblical witness itself would seem to cast doubt on such a conviction. God's prophets quite frequently provoked persecution and condemnation from the holy community. Jesus himself did not always meet with acceptance from the community's 'powers-that-be' for his particular interpretation of received tradition. So who decides what is 'individualistic interpretation' and what are the boundaries of 'the life of the Church' within which the sacred text must be read? Is it not wise, at least sometimes, to attend to voices from the edge – and, indeed, from 'outside the camp'? Does 'Church of God' in effect mean those in positions of authority therein? Engagement with such questions is important for any faith community – and for its critical friends.

In paragraph 25, *The Gift of Authority* argues that: 'Fresh recourse to Tradition in a new situation is the means by which God's revelation in Christ is recalled. This is assisted by the insights of biblical scholars and theologians and the wisdom of holy persons.' In the light of what has been said earlier, how free are such 'assistants' to pursue their enquiries within the integrity of their own disciplines? The process of 're-reception' may face 'the Church' with highly uncomfortable challenge.

Having stressed that the Scriptures emerged from and are related to specific contexts, *The Gift of Authority* (in common with other dialogues) does not work out the implications of this when making use of scriptural references in the text as a whole. This is certainly true of its key biblical text, 2 Corinthians 1.19-20. It is extracted from its Pauline context (Paul defending himself and his proclamation of the gospel) and applied to the various matters to do with authority raised in the statement. There is, to say the least, a debate to be had as to whether Paul's words can be stretched that far. There is also a danger, if this line of thinking is pushed to extremes, that the 'Amen' of the people becomes merely compliant acquiescence.

This would hardly be in line with the biblical record where, again and again, the 'Amen' of communities and individuals (Paul included) comes only through struggle. As God's 'yes' in Jesus Christ is no easy affirmation, so a responsive 'Amen' is no painless reflex. On both sides, it brings wound as well as blessing.

Another biblical theme that has been widely exploited in recent dialogues is that of *koinonia* (communion). A significant New Testament reflection on the life of the people of God has become a focal means of interpretation for ecclesiology and an impetus towards ecumenism. Yet the dialogues contain very little by way of critical examination of the precise usage of *koinonia* in the Scriptures. So Meissen, paragraph 4, for example, sees the 'reality of a *koinonia*' as 'underlying many of the NT descriptions of the Church', perceiving this as a 'sharing in the life of the Holy Trinity and therein with our fellow-members of the Church'. But no scriptural references are given to support this. In the official ecumenical texts generally, there is hardly any exploration as to whether the biblical material can bear the loading put upon it; or, indeed, whether it requires a wider and deeper interpretation than that already given. Perhaps, to use *The Gift of Authority*'s terminology, *koinonia* is an insight which needs to be 're-received'.

C some summary matters arising

Even this brief analysis of ecumenical texts clearly indicates that there are still major issues relating to Scripture which need to be explored more openly and more searchingly as the quest for full visible unity continues.

All the dialogues regard the Bible as normative and fundamentally authoritative. What is lacking, however, is a sustained exploration of what this might mean, and how the range of terminology used might be understood. A word like 'inspired', for instance, can have a variety of senses, depending on context and assumptions.

It is interesting that, though the concept of inspiration is present in many of the texts, the Holy Spirit seems to be accorded a somewhat low profile as regards the formation and interpretation of Scripture. Invariably, a Christocentric approach is adopted. The Bible bears witness to the word and work of God in Christ. The New Testament treats directly of this; the Old Testament is to be seen in its light.[20]

The role of the Holy Spirit in relation to Scripture would thus seem ripe for exploration in ecumenical exchange. In particular, what might it mean for the interpretative task that the Holy Spirit leads into all truth? And if the Spirit still moves where it wills, what might be the implications of this for discerning who could be conveying the messages of Scripture in this age and in its manifold cultural expressions? Can the Spirit really be contained within the constituency of 'Church authorities', however defined?

Beyond the highlighting of issues of interpretation by some, none of the dialogues really engages with the world of critical scholarship and hermeneutics. The 'proof-text' method is extensively employed. Perhaps, amongst other things, this points to the need for more biblical scholars to be involved in the endeavour of ecumenical dialogue. The enterprise does seem to have a predominance of participants from other theological disciplines.

How the Bible is understood and used tends to be carried forward from one dialogue to another. As a method, this has the advantage of affirming and appropriating what has been agreed. It does mean, however, that the opportunity is lessened to approach things in a fresh way.

Major questions having major implications are not often addressed in a direct way. So, for example: Who should interpret Scripture? Where are the limits of interpretation and who determines them? Where are the controls? What methods of interpretation are appropriate and how might they be worked out in the context of ecumenical dialogue? Is the Bible a closed book? In what relation should it stand with the whole body of Christian tradition down the ages – and with the experience of living in our present age?

Questions such as these point to the need for ecumenical partners to explore the Scriptures (and their significance) together.
In studying the Bible together, in the contexts of worship, devotion and dialogue, the matters raised above could be opened up and attended to. That is no easy task, but therein lies the opportunity for some deep healing of memories, as well as an impetus towards the more effective proclamation of the gospel in this generation. Such concerns, surely, bring us very near the heart of the matter.

D some observations

Article VI of the Thirty-Nine Articles of the Church of England states that:

Holy Scripture containeth all things necessary to salvation: so that whatsoever is not read therein, nor may be proved thereby, is not to be required of any man, that it should be believed as an article of the Faith, or be thought requisite or necessary to salvation.

But how are these 'things necessary to salvation' to be identified, understood and interpreted? Paying more attention to widely accepted Anglican approaches to this question might have particular pertinence for the ecumenical endeavour.

The pastoral letter on 'The Reading of Scripture' issued by bishops of the Anglican Communion gathered for the Lambeth Conference of 1988 put it thus:

6 We affirm that the Scriptures are best seen as the Church's books – a body of writing which, for the earliest Christian communities, defined the Word which they had received and by which the Church lives. Through the ages the living and growing 'mind' of the Church has best been formed when the Church has been attentive to the scriptural word within the context of its liturgy, prayer and communal life. Whether as bishops at the Lambeth Conference or as a local congregation, any Christian community is called to be attentive to Scripture and to interpret it in the light of its own situation.

7 Such interpretation takes place in a number of ways:

- in the public and private reading of Scripture
- through preaching and teaching
- in small group study
- through the work of scholars who engage the horizon of the Bible with that of the contemporary world
- by its application in the daily lives of Christian men and women.

The meaning of Scripture must be, in fact always is, declared and explained within changing circumstances, cultural settings and languages. Scripture must not be made to serve the ends of a particular culture nor be tied too closely to scholarly trends, nor must it be read apart from the particular experiences of people. Discernment is the process through which a body of believers *receives* the Word of God in its own time and context.

8 The disciplined daily reading and study of Scripture and a searching of the accumulated 'mind' of the Church's tradition enabled us at the Lambeth Conference to address a wide range

of issues confronting Christians around the globe. We commend this pattern to you, our sisters and brothers in local communities of faith. The task of declaring, explaining and living God's message belongs to the whole people of God. We invite you to join us in a process such as we have been privileged to share – waiting upon God, studying God's word in a reflective way, taking care to listen to those fellow believers whose life and experiences differ from ours, and making broad use of resources of interpretation.

9 Together, let us wait on the Word of God in prayer and expectation.[21]

The report of the Inter-Anglican Theological and Doctrinal Commission (*The Virginia Report*)[22] in addressing issues of communion and diversity within Anglicanism (very significant also, of course, in the search for full visible unity in the wider Church of God) recalls and emphasizes the classic interplay in Anglican life between Scripture, tradition and reason:

> Anglicans affirm the sovereign authority of the Holy Scriptures as the medium through which God by the Spirit communicates his word in the Church and thus enables people to respond with understanding and faith. The Scriptures are 'uniquely inspired witness to divine revelation,' and 'the primary norm for Christian faith and life.'

> The Scriptures, however, must be translated, read, and understood, and their meaning grasped through a continuing process of interpretation. Since the seventeenth century, Anglicans have held that Scripture is to be understood and read in the light afforded by the contexts of 'tradition' and 'reason'.[23]

Tradition, as understood by *The Virginia Report*, refers primarily to the Scriptures themselves, 'in that they embody "the tradition," "the message," "the faith once delivered to the saints"'. But that fundamental tradition is by no means a static proposition:

> Tradition refers to the ongoing Spirit-led life of the Church which receives, and in receiving interprets afresh God's abiding message . . . Tradition is not to be understood as an accumulation of formulae and texts but the living mind, the nerve centre of the Church.[24]

Regarding 'reason', *The Virginia Report* says this:

> Anglicanism sees reason in the sense of the 'mind' of the culture in which the Church lives and the Gospel is proclaimed,

as a legitimate instrument for the interpretation of God's message in the Scriptures. Sometimes Scriptures affirm the new insights of a particular age or culture, sometimes they challenge or contradict those insights.[25]

The implications of this approach are that

the characteristic Anglican way of living with a constant dynamic interplay of Scripture, tradition and reason means that the mind of God has constantly to be discerned afresh, not only in every age, but in each and every context.[26]

The Virginia Report also reminds us that

The Scriptures are read and interpreted in the round of common daily prayer and in the celebration of the sacraments . . . (p. 33)

It is a timely reminder. The written Word is there to point to the Word made flesh.

E coda

In his poem 'Little Gidding', T. S. Eliot writes

We shall not cease from exploration
And the end of all our exploring
Will be to arrive where we started
And to know the place for the first time.

However we deal with Scripture, whether in using it liturgically, pastorally, academically, personally, in seeking common ground within the Churches, or in other ways, we are for ever dealing with 'a treasury of most costly jewels'. As together we go on exploring the ground of our unity in Christ, may we continually discover new insights and new ways of together owning and sharing this treasury.

(NB Part I was prepared for a separate occasion in a different context and therefore remains the copyright material of the Ven. Dr Joy Tetley.)

Appendix

Ecumenical dialogue: specific biblical references in key documents

Together in Mission and Ministry (Porvoo Common Statement)

God's Kingdom and the Mystery and Purpose of the Church
paras *14–20*

Col 1.19-27	18
1 John 1.3	15
1 John 4.14	18
John 1.1-13	16
John 3.16-18	15
John 3.17	18
Rom 6.1-11	15, 17
Rom 8.14-17	15
Rom 8.19-22	14
1 Cor 10.16,17	17
1 Cor 12,13	17
2 Cor 5.17-19	14
Gal 4.5	15
Eph 1.9,10	14
Eph 1.10	18
Eph 2.8	16
Eph 2.14	18
Eph 2.19,20	14

The Nature of Communion and the Goal of Unity
paras *21–28*

John 17.21	21
Acts 2.41,42	24
Acts 15	25
1 Cor 1.11-13	27
2 Cor 5	27
Eph 1	27
Eph 4.4-6	21
Phil 2.2	28
1 John 1.1-10	21
1 John 2.18,19	27

What we agree in faith
paras *29–33*

Col 1.20	32l
1 Pet 2.5	32i

Episcopacy in the service of the Apostolicity of the Church
paras *34–57*

Isa 11.1-31	47
1 Cor 12.4-11	38
Eph 1.23	54
Eph 3.17-19	54
Eph 4.11-13	38

Called to Witness and Service (Reuilly Common Statement)

Church as Sign, Instrument and Foretaste . . .
paras *16–18*

Gen 12.1-3	17
Isa 49.6	17
2 Cor 5.19	17
Eph 1.3,9,10	17
Eph 4.7,11-13	17
Col 1.15-20	17

The Church as Communion
paras *19–20*

1 John 1.3,4	19

Growth towards full Visible Unity
paras *21–29*

Heb 13.8	25

Agreement in Faith
paras *30–32*

1 Pet 2.5	31h

Apostolicity of the Church and Ministry
paras *33–40*

Mark 10.42-45	34
John 13.1-17	34
2 Cor 1.24	34
Phil 2.1-11	34
1 Pet 5.1-5	34

The Gift of Authority

God's Reign and Our Unity (International Anglican–Lutheran Dialogue, 1984)

Our task		*Acts 1.22*	48
paras 1–24		Acts 2.38	51
		Acts 10.37	48
John 12.32	17	Rom 6.1-11	52
John 17.21	17	Rom 6.3	50
Eph 1.10	14, 17	Rom 6.3ff	55
Col 1.19f	17	Rom 6.5	50
Col 1.20	18	Rom 8.14-17	51
		1 Cor 4.1	69
		1 Cor 6.11	55
God's apostolic people		1 Cor 11.26	69
paras 25–38		1 Cor 11.17-32	70
		1 Cor 12.13	47, 51
Matt 11.27	25	2 Cor 4.7-15	52
John 10.30	25	2 Cor 5.14f	60
John 15.26	25, 38	2 Cor 5.18	69
John 16.8-11	38	2 Cor 5.18-21	60
John 16.12-15	38	2 Cor 5.21	48
John 17.21	25, 27	Gal 3.27f	47, 51
John 20.19-23	26	Eph 4.4f	47
Rom 15.7	27	Col 1.22	45
1 Cor 1.13	27	Col 3.12	55
Eph 2.7	27	Col 3.16	45
Eph 2.16	27	Titus 3.5	55
Eph 4.15,16	31	Heb 10.19ff	64
Col 1.15-23	26		
Col 2.19	26		
Col 3.11	26	*Ministry in the Church*	
Heb 11.10	35	paras 73–104	
		Matt 28.19	75
Life in the Church		Matt 28.19f	76
paras 39–72		Mark 3.14f	73
		John 10.7-15	78
Ex 12.11	63	John 20.19-23	73
Isa 42.1ff	50	John 21.15-19	78
Matt 28.19ff	53	1 Cor 11.17-22	81
Mark 1.1	48	Eph 4.12f	92
Mark 3.27	49	1 Pet 2.5, 9	79
Mark 10.38	50	1 Pet 4.10	81
Luke 12.50	50		
Luke 24.35	64		
John 7.39	51	*Our Goal*	
John 12.31	49	paras 105–124	
John 13.36	64		
John 14.1-6	64	Ex 14.15	124
John 17.18	64	Acts 9.31	105
John 17.19	64	Heb 3.12-19	124
John 17.21	43		
John 20.22,23	51		

ARCIC, *The Final Report*, 1982

Preface	
Rom 5.5	4
Phil 3.13	1
1 John 1.3	3

Introduction	
John 11.52	6
John 17.20ff	6
Rom 8.15	5
2 Cor 5.18	6
Gal 4.6	5
Eph 2.14	6
1 John 1.3	5

Eucharistic Doctrine	
Statement paras 1–12	
1 Cor 15.28	5

Elucidation paras 1–10	
Luke 22.19	5
1 Cor 11.24,25	5

Ministry and Ordination	
Statement paras 1–17	
Matt 28.19	4
Mark 3.14	4
Mark 10.43-45	6
Acts 6.4	10

Acts 20.28	6
Rom 12.1	13
2 Cor 3.5,6	14
Eph 4.11-13	5
1 Tim 4.12-16	6
1 Pet 2.9	13
1 Pet 5.1-4	6

Elucidation paras 1–6	
Acts 14.23	4
1 Pet 2.5	2

Authority in the Church I	
Statement paras 1–26	
Matt 16.18,19	24
Matt 18.20	16
Luke 22.31,32	24
John 17.11	11
John 17.21	11
John 21.15-17	24
Acts 2.42	5
Acts 15	9
Acts 15.28	16
1 Cor 12.4-11	5
Eph 4.11,12	5

Elucidation paras 1–8	
Heb 1.1-3	2

Authority in the Church II	
Matt 16.16	3
Matt 16.18	3, 4
Matt 16.19	4
Matt 18.18	4
Mark 8.29	3
Luke 6.14	5
Luke 9.20	3
Luke 22.24ff	5
Luke 22.31, 32	3
Luke 22.32	5
Luke 24.34	3
John 6.69	3
John 21.15-17	5
John 21.16,17	3
Acts 1.2-8	4
Acts 1.21, 22	8
Acts 3.15	3
Acts 10.41	3
Acts 11.1-18	5
Acts 15	3
1 Cor 9.1	4
1 Cor 15.5	3
Gal 1.18, 19	3
Gal 2.7, 8	4
Gal 2.11	3
Gal 2.11-14	5
Eph 2.20	4

The Meissen Agreement

I The Church as sign . . .	
Gen 12.1-3	2
Isa 49.6	2
2 Cor 5.19	2
Eph 1.3,9,10	2
Eph 4.7,11-13	2
Col 1.15-20	2

II The Church as koinonia

None

III Growth towards full, visible unity	
None	

IV Communion already shared

None

V Agreement in faith	
Col 1.20	15

VI Mutual acknowledgement . . .

None

The Fetter Lane Common Statement (Church of England – Moravian Church)

Foreword	Eph 1.7	20	V Apostolicity and
	Eph 4.7, 11-13	20	succession
John 17.22	7	Col 1.15-20	20	paras 41–48

John 17.18   41

I Our shared past and present	III What we can now agree in faith	VI Issues still to be faced
paras 1–18	para 28	paras 49–54
None	Col 1.20 28g	None

II Our common calling to full, visible unity	IV The ordained ministry of the Church	VII Our common future
paras 19–27	paras 29–40	para 55
2 Cor 5.19 20	None	None
Eph 1.3, 9, 10 20		

Apostolicity and Succession (House of Bishops of the Church of England)

Introduction	Apostolic Ministry . . .
paras 1–15	paras 43–51

Rom 12.4-8	3	None
1 Cor 12.4-31	3	
2 Cor 5.18,19	3	
Eph 4.1-16	3, 4	Episcopacy and
Col 1.16	3	Succession
		paras 52–67

The Apostolicity of the Church	Matt 18.20	52
paras 16–33	Matt 28.20	52

Matt 16.18	29	Towards Greater Unity
John 8.31-33	29	paras 68–76
John 17.14	20	
		References are all from Porvoo – already
Signs of Apostolicity		covered.
paras 34–42		

None

chapter five

'according to the Scriptures ...': the use of the Bible in *Baptism, Eucharist and Ministry*

Paula Gooder

introduction

The Lima text (1982) otherwise known as *Baptism, Eucharist and Ministry* (BEM)[1] had a much wider impact on the worldwide Christian community than had been anticipated. The statement on BEM made by the Faith and Order Commission in Budapest, 1989 noted that it had become 'the most widely distributed, translated, and discussed ecumenical text in modern times'.[2] BEM's significance lies not only in the fact that its reflection of 'a large measure of agreement' between the members of the Commission is 'unprecedented in the modern ecumenical movement'[3] but also in the way that it continues to shape and inform contemporary ecumenical debate. BEM both reflects the ecumenical method established in the 1980s by the Faith and Order Commission and shapes future use of such method.

As well as its importance as a text which reflects ecumenical method in general, BEM also arose at a time of particular importance in the debate about the use of the Bible in the ecumenical process. As a result it illustrates well some of the principles that lie behind the use of the Bible in a text such as this, but also raises various issues which the Faith and Order Commission has gone on to explore in more detail.

This chapter explores the use of the Bible in BEM, looking at the context from which it arose and the ways in which it uses the Bible to shape its argument. It would be wrong to begin such a study without an acknowledgement of the profoundly positive aspects of BEM's use of the Bible. The text is firmly rooted in the Bible and this is evident in every paragraph of the document.

Having said this, within the ecumenical world BEM was breaking new ground in its use of the Bible, as will become clear below. As a result, various problems arose that need evaluation.

This chapter begins and ends by placing BEM in its historical context, at the start, in the context of ecumenical debate on the use of the Bible, and at the end, in the context of hermeneutical method in biblical scholarship. Between these two historical concerns, the study looks at the different ways in which the Bible is used in BEM and the strengths and weaknesses of these uses. It ends by reflecting on the lessons that can be learnt from BEM for future ecumenical documents that seek to root themselves in the Bible.

a brief history of biblical hermeneutics in ecumenical debate

It is hardly surprising that attitudes towards the Bible within ecumenical debate are complex. On the one hand it is regarded as being a symbol of unity. In the first world conference on Faith and Order in Lausanne, 1927, it was stated that despite 'the differences in doctrine among us, we are united in a common Christian faith which is proclaimed in the holy scriptures'.[4] On the other hand, however, the interpretation of the Bible is one of the most hotly disputed subjects within ecumenism.

This dual role of the Bible as the embodiment both of unity and of difference between different groups within Christianity is reflected in the various world conferences. As noted already, the first world conference at Lausanne set out the significance of the Bible within ecumenical debate. In the following two world conferences in 1937 at Edinburgh and in 1952 at Lund, it was the differences between denominations in the interpretation of the Bible that began to come to the fore. Statements from both conferences focus on the differences that exist in attitudes to the Bible.[5]

It was only in 1963, at the fourth world conference in Montreal, that what is widely regarded as a significant breakthrough occurred. Following this conference a statement was made on the relationship between Scripture and Tradition which has had a great influence on subsequent ecumenical debate:

> Our starting point is that we are all living in a tradition which goes back to our Lord and has its roots in the Old Testament, and are all indebted to that tradition inasmuch as we have received the revealed truth, the gospel, through its being

transmitted from one generation to another. Thus we can say that we exist as Christians by the Tradition of the gospel (the paradosis of the kerygma) testified in scripture, transmitted in and by the church through the power of the Holy Spirit.[6] So important was this statement that part of it ('the Tradition . . . the Holy Spirit') became included in the preface to BEM.[7] Following this, various other reports on hermeneutics were produced at Bristol in 1967, at Louvain in 1971 and at Bangalore in 1978.[8]

It was against this background that BEM was written and to a certain extent BEM is an attempt to reflect a practical working out of the Montreal statement. As often happens in such circumstances, BEM 'raised as many hermeneutical questions as it answered'[9] and set a chain of further study in motion. *A Treasure in Earthen Vessels*[10] and the volume of essays published to support and reflect upon it[11] are the most recent products of this study.

The use of the Bible in BEM, therefore, can only properly be understood against the background of a process of study into hermeneutics in ecumenical debate. It is an important staging post along the way, but not an end product. It reflects certain achievements in ecumenical debate but in its turn raises many more.

the place of the Bible in BEM

Max Thurian claims that BEM 'is founded on the word of God', going on to say that this is 'its deepest intention'.[12] This is immediately evident from the start of two of its three major sections. The section on baptism begins: 'Christian baptism is rooted in the ministry of Jesus of Nazareth, in his death and resurrection'[13] and sets this against a background of biblical language, noting that 'it is entry into the New Covenant', that it is a 'gift of God' and is 'administered in the name of the Father Son and Holy Spirit', going on to cite the famous passage Matthew 28.18-20.

The next section, Eucharist, begins even more firmly based upon the Bible with an extensive quotation from 1 Corinthians 11.23-25, which is the Pauline account of the institution of the Last Supper. The third section does not begin so overtly within the biblical tradition, using what might be regarded as more theological language than biblical language: 'In a broken world God calls the whole of humanity to become God's people'.[14] It is only later within this section that the Bible is drawn back into the debate about the nature of ministry.

These three, slightly different, beginnings to the three major sections illustrate well the variety of method employed within BEM. Sometimes the Bible is quoted directly as the starting point for the discussion, as it is at the beginning of the section on Eucharist. At other times biblical references are given (but not quoted) to support a point being made or language is used which is evidently drawn from the biblical tradition but is not quoted directly, as happens at the start of the baptism section. At other times again, debate is begun on theological grounds and the Bible is drawn in later when relevant to the debate, as at the start of the ministry section.

These different ways of using the Bible are evident throughout the document and not just at the start of each of the sections. Tabbernee identifies five different ways in which the Bible has been used in BEM, which include these three and add a further two: direct biblical quotations, biblical citations, biblical allusions, biblical concepts, and biblical terminology.[15] In these it is possible to discern the influence of the Montreal statement but also to note where problems in the implementation of the statement begin to arise.

biblical allusions

This is probably the most straightforward of the uses of the Bible found in BEM. Throughout the document the language used shows that it has been drawn from the biblical tradition. Although not direct quotations, these allusions give strong evidence that the authors of the text are thoroughly steeped in the biblical writings and support the Montreal statement 'that we exist as Christians by the Tradition of the gospel (the paradosis of the kerygma) testified in scripture'.[16]

A good example of this can be found in 'E. The Sign of the Kingdom' in the second section of the baptism part of the document.[17] This section reads:

> Baptism initiates the reality of the new life given in the midst of the present world. It gives participation in the community of the Holy Spirit. It is a sign of the Kingdom of God and of the life of the world to come. Through the gifts of faith, hope and love, baptism has a dynamic which embraces the whole of life, extends to all nations, and anticipates the day when every tongue will confess that Jesus is Lord to the glory of God the Father.

This passage alludes to various different parts of the New Testament, many, though not all of them, from the Pauline corpus. The reference to new life in the first sentence evokes Paul's statement in Romans 7.6 that we are now slaves 'in the new life of the Spirit'. The reference to participation in the community of the Holy Spirit is reminiscent of the many times that Paul speaks of membership of the body of Christ in the Spirit, the most famous example of which is 1 Corinthians 12.13: 'in the one Spirit we were all baptized into one body'. The language of the kingdom of God is, of course, from the Jesus tradition in the Gospels of Mark and Luke. However, in the second half of this sentence the use of the phrase 'life of the world to come' is intriguing, as although the sentiment is familiar from the biblical tradition the wording is not. This phrase comes not from the Bible but from Jewish tradition and is a translation of the Hebrew phrase *ha'olam haba'*.[18] This refers to an eschatological expectation which is similar to but not exactly the same as Revelation's 'new heaven and new earth' (Revelation 21.1). It is a convenient shorthand but not actually a biblical allusion. This same shorthand is used at the end of the Nicene Creed: 'We look for the resurrection of the dead and the life of the world to come'. It is likely that the use of the phrase here is a reference not to the Bible but to this part of the Nicene Creed.

The final sentence of this section incorporates two well-known Pauline phrases. The first, 'faith, hope and love', is taken directly from 1 Corinthians 13.13 and the other, 'every tongue will confess that Jesus is Lord to the glory of God the Father', is from Philippians 2.11.

The value of this approach is that it demonstrates in a very practical way the truth of the Montreal statement 'that we exist as Christians by the Tradition of the gospel . . . testified in scripture',[19] since it demonstrates that even the language Christians use to speak of themselves is steeped with this Tradition. However, this approach should be employed with caution.

One factor that becomes apparent, both in this short excerpt from BEM and in the document as a whole, is that biblical allusions are more readily drawn from the Pauline corpus than from any other section of the Bible. Although direct quotations are slightly more evenly balanced, as we shall see below, the phrases that have most deeply affected contemporary Christian language are Pauline. The danger of this is an implicit bias to a certain strand of early Christian tradition at the expense of the whole. This raises issues about a dependence upon one part of the Bible rather than the whole canon, to which we shall return later.

A second danger was also illustrated by section E, 'The Sign of the Kingdom'. The problem of using biblical allusion without reference is that phrases may be used which are not actually from the canon of Scripture. It can often be difficult to work out the source of a particular phrase and hence the context from which it arises.

biblical concepts and biblical terminology

Very similar to biblical allusions is the use of biblical concepts and biblical terminology. These two occur regularly in BEM and the difference between them is that the biblical concepts include ideas such as the new covenant, grace of God, reconciliation; whereas biblical terminology uses words, often in Greek, to refer to a specific idea such as *anamnesis, parousia* and *epiklesis*. While both biblical concepts and terminology find their origins in the Bible, they have often come to have a much greater meaning in subsequent Christian theology. For example, although cognates of the word *epiklesis* do occur in the Bible, that precise form does not occur nor do its cognates mean quite what it is understood to mean in a eucharistic context.

For this reason, the use of biblical concepts and terminology does not quite fit into the category of use of the Bible. Their use is often more indirect than that. They might be found in some form in the biblical tradition but have gained their significance and much of their meaning in subsequent Christian thinking. Biblical concepts and terminology have an important function in documents such as BEM but not as examples of direct biblical hermeneutics.

biblical quotations

A major criticism of BEM's use of the Bible has been that it can, at times, appear to be 'prooftexting', that is, pulling Scripture out of context to support a point made. This is especially true when looking at its use of quotations from the Bible. Generally speaking, when quotations are given they are taken out of their original context. An example of this can be found in the ministry section of the document which claims that the 'Twelve were promised that they would "sit on thrones judging the tribes of Israel" (Luke 22.30)'.[20] This quotation occurs in a section unique to Luke in which the disciples are disputing which one of them is to be regarded as the greatest, though none of this is reflected in BEM.

Various writers have defended BEM rigorously against the charge of prooftexting. M. Thurian argues that there 'is no question . . . of a simplistic biblicism treating scripture as if it were an untouchable law'.[21] W. Tabbernee maintains in relation to the use of 1 Corinthians 11.23-25 at the start of the section on Eucharist that this approach 'is not a form of "prooftexting" but a very effective use of the historical critical method'.[22] Nevertheless various issues are raised by this criticism, which need to be addressed.

A defence of this approach can be mounted on two levels. A first consideration is that quotations given within BEM are not entirely out of context. Rather they are cited against the background of the extensive biblical allusion that we noted in the previous section. The overall impression of BEM is of a text rooted in and shaped by biblical ideas and language. It is unfair therefore to accuse it of plucking texts entirely out of context. A biblical context is given in the text itself by the biblical allusions woven throughout the document.

A second defence is that at times BEM does reflect knowledge and use of biblical scholarship in its use of quotations. As Tabbernee points out, the choice of 1 Corinthians 11.23-25 reflects the influence of biblical scholarship since this is widely acknowledged to be the earliest written account of the institution of the Last Supper.

Having said this, however, a problem remains which was noted in many of the responses to BEM. The Report on the Process and Responses to BEM stated that although the 'use of the *scriptures* was generally and widely appreciated . . . a number of comments noted a lack of differentiation in the citations and sensed a lack of awareness of underlying exegetical issues'.[23] This is a hermeneutical problem. BEM appears to assume that the Bible has a single opinion on issues, which can be supported by a biblical reference and which speaks into a single context. Biblical scholarship has demonstrated that, in many instances, this cannot be upheld.

The biblical authors themselves were writing in and to different contexts and consequently had different opinions. Sometimes these are blatant disagreements. A very obvious example of this can be found within the Old Testament. The prophet Nehemiah forbade intermarriage between the Judahites and the surrounding nations of Ashdod, Ammon and Moab (Nehemiah 13.23). Whereas the book of Ruth maintains that Ruth, a Moabite, was an ancestor of King David (Ruth 4.17; Matthew 1.5). More often, however, the differences between, and even sometimes within, texts are more subtle and require detailed exegesis to understand them. An example of this is Paul's statement about women in 1 Corinthians 11 and 14. In the first he appears to say that women can speak during worship provided that their heads are covered (11.5); whereas later he seems to say that they cannot speak at all (14.34). Simply citing a verse does not do justice to these complex exegetical issues.

An appreciation of the diversity of the Bible and of the contexts of its readers is very much clearer in the more recent document *A Treasure in Earthen Vessels*, though how this appreciation of diversity would be illustrated in a more practical paper like BEM remains to be seen.

biblical citations

A technique closely linked to the use of biblical quotations is that of giving biblical references to support points made elsewhere. This is the most common use of the Bible in BEM with just over sixty references to various biblical passages. This practice was also criticized in the responses to BEM. The Report on the Process and Responses to BEM states that some responses 'criticize that the scriptures have not always been allowed to function as the centre and norm of the faith'.[24] In other words, points are made which are only later supported by biblical texts, rather than allowing the biblical text to shape these points in the first place.

A similar defence might be mounted against this criticism as against the criticism of prooftexting. In many cases, positions stated in BEM have indeed been shaped by the biblical text over long periods of history. The fact that the workings that have led up to the adoption of a certain position have not been shown does not mean that they do not exist. This is true for all ecumenical documents. Normally only a final snapshot of the conclusions from a debate can be revealed in publication. This can often obscure the fact that complex, sophisticated discussion has taken place in the process that leads up to this publication. Indeed, Tabbernee maintains that 'the editors of the Lima text presuppose a certain amount of biblical literacy on the part of their readers'.[25] Thus explaining why they opted to refer in passing to biblical texts rather than to explain them in full. Nevertheless, fair or otherwise, there are times when the impression remains that biblical passages have been chosen to support an idea rather than as the source out of which that idea grew. Whatever the intention of the editors, this can come dangerously close to 'prooftexting'.

the choice of passages used in BEM

The choice of biblical passages within any ecumenical document is interesting since it reveals which texts have influenced the writers more than others. We noted above that the Pauline corpus has influenced the language and phraseology of BEM more than any other tradition within the Bible. A further exploration of the passages actually cited, rather than just alluded to, is even more illuminating.

To begin with, there are many more citations of biblical references in the baptism section than in either the Eucharist or ministry sections (there are about 38 biblical references in the baptism section as opposed to 18 in the Eucharist section and 20 in the ministry section). This seems to reveal a greater dependence upon the Bible in the discussion of baptism than in the other two sections.

the use of the Old Testament

Also of significance is the scarcity of direct reference to the Old Testament. There are very few references to the Old Testament in the whole of the document. In the section on baptism the reference to the Old Testament is left vague. In talking about the various images of baptism in the New Testament, BEM states that these 'images are sometimes linked with the symbolic uses of water in the Old Testament'.[26] The vagueness of the phrase makes it somewhat frustrating, as it does not state who makes this connection – the biblical writers or subsequent interpreters – nor does it give examples of the symbolic uses of water that it has in mind. A similar reference is made in the section on ministry to God's choosing of Israel;[27] again the reference is so vague that it is hard to see what it means in this context.

The other two references in the Eucharist section are slightly clearer since the text makes reference to 'the Passover memorial of Israel's deliverance from the land of bondage' and to 'the meal of the Covenant on Mount Sinai (Ex 24)'.[28] However, this reference to the Covenant meal is problematic, as it seems to imply that the whole chapter describes a covenant meal. In fact it does not. Exodus 24 is one of the most complex chapters in the book of Exodus. The majority of source critics propose that it is made up of three different sources with verses 1-2 and 9-11 from one source (J) referring to a covenant meal, verses 3-8 from another (E) referring to the sprinkling of blood as part of the covenant ratification, and verses 15-18 from a third source (P) and describing a theophany.[29]

It is somewhat surprising that the Old Testament has so small a role in the document and, when it is mentioned, that the references are as vague as they are. This is the weakest feature of BEM's use of the Bible, especially in the light of its dependence on the Montreal statement, which says that 'Our starting point is that we are all living in a tradition which goes back to our Lord and has its roots in the Old Testament.' These roots are not so apparent in BEM as they might be. This follows a trend within many Christian communities to focus on the New Testament almost to the exclusion of the Old but which results in an impoverishment of the Christian faith. There are many texts from the Old Testament that could have provided a very helpful biblical background for the discussion in BEM. For example, the crossing of the Red Sea, the entry into the Promised Land or Naaman's healing by immersion in the river of Jordan might all have been drawn out as a background to baptism. The cyclical nature of history, which saw redemption occurring over and over again and which allowed the Israelites to understand the return from exile as a new exodus, might have provided a helpful insight into the concept of anamnesis, or examples of prophetic and other calling might have been used to illustrate God's calling in the ministry section.

In the section on biblical allusions above, we noted the bias in BEM towards the Pauline corpus in the use of language to speak about Christianity. Add to this the scarcity of references to the Old Testament and questions about the use of the canon of Scripture begin to emerge. Use of the Bible often produces a *de facto* canon within a canon. This is natural but should be resisted at all costs. It is important within ecumenical debate to demonstrate, in practice as well as in theory, an acceptance and use of the whole canon both as a reflection of the beliefs of the member Churches but also as a model of good practice for their members.

the use of certain New Testament passages

In striking contrast to the way in which the Old Testament is used in BEM, various New Testament passages are used regularly. Particular favourites are: the Matthean and Pauline accounts of the institution of the last supper (Matthew 26.26-29 and 1 Corinthians 11.20-25, three times each); the great commission in Matthew (28.18-20, twice); Paul's discussion of baptism (Romans 6.3-11, three times); the Ephesians passage which mentions the 'pledge of our inheritance' (Ephesians 1.13-14, twice) and the Petrine passage about the purpose of baptism (1 Peter 3.20-21, twice). One passage, however, stands out because it is used so often – six times in all, four times in the baptism section and once each in the other two sections. This passage is Galatians 3.27-28 (in the baptism section, 3.27 is cited once on its own and 3.27-28 three times; in the Eucharist and ministry sections only 3.28 is cited):

[27]As many of you as were baptized into Christ have clothed yourselves with Christ. [28]There is no longer Jew or Greek, there is no longer slave or free, there is no longer male and female; for all of you are one in Christ Jesus.

On one level this is hardly surprising, as these verses are among the most well known and well used verses in the New Testament. Nevertheless their use in BEM illustrates well some of the problems that can arise from the technique of biblical citation. The frequent use of Galatians 3.27–28 requires the text to bear a lot of theological weight. This passage is cited to illustrate:

1. re-clothing in Christ,[30]

2. 'a new humanity in which barriers of division whether of sex or race or social status are transcended',[31]

3. 'the genuine baptismal unity of the Christian community',[32]

4. 'that baptism into Christ's death ... motivate[s] Christians to strive for the realization of the will of God in all realms of life',[33]

5. the need to search for 'appropriate relationships in social, economic and political life',[34]

6. that there is in Christ 'no male or female'.[35]

Some of these seem to be more obvious uses of the passage than others. Uses one and three fit well as Galatians 3.27-28 is explicitly about baptism, though other passages could have been used instead to avoid undue repetition. For example, Romans 13.14 ('put on the Lord Jesus Christ') could have been used to illustrate being re-clothed in Christ, and 1 Corinthians 12.13 ('For in the one Spirit we were all baptized into one body') might have expressed genuine baptismal unity slightly better.

The crucial issue, however, is what views Galatians 3.27-28 can, legitimately, be used to support. The passage is widely regarded as being an early Christian, possibly pre-Pauline baptismal formula.[36] An important interpretational question, therefore, is whether the unity described by this passage refers to the Christian community in general[37] or to the situation of baptism in particular.[38] If it is the latter, then what Paul is referring to here is not the status of Christians within the Christian community but how they achieve access to it. In other words it does not matter if you were a Jew or a Gentile, slave or free, male and female before, what matters is being baptized into Christ. It may not be a passage about how Christians relate to each other within the body of Christ but how they enter that body.

The attractiveness of interpreting the passage in this way is that it makes sense of places elsewhere in Paul in which it becomes very clear that there is a difference between slave and free, or between male and female because they are required to act in different ways – the slave in subjection to his or her master and the wife to her husband. An interesting additional argument that Witherington makes here is that detailed attention should be paid to the wording of Galatians 3.28, which states that there is neither Jew nor Greek, slave nor free, nor male *and* female. This he suggests refers not to gender but to marital status.[39]

If Witherington's interpretation of the passage is correct, then Galatians 3.28 cannot really be used to support statements about a new humanity, the need for appropriate relationships nor to argue that there is no male or female in Christ. The fourth use of the passage ('that baptism into Christ's death . . . motivate[s] Christians to strive for the realization of the will of God in all realms of life') is something of a puzzle as it is not entirely clear why Galatians 3.27-28 supports this phrase. Unlike Romans 6.9ff. and 1 Peter 2.21 – 4.6 cited alongside it, the Galatians passage states a fact (that all *are* one) rather than something which is to be achieved by the Christian community.

The use of Galatians 3.27-28 in BEM cautions against the natural tendency to have a favourite passage which is used regularly. Passages can only be used to support a point if they genuinely mean what the writers of a document want them to mean. The overuse of Galatians 3.27-28 in BEM dilutes its value as a revolutionary early text within Christianity because it has been made to mean too much.

hermeneutical method and BEM

It is hard, in a document like BEM, to discern the hermeneutical method that lies behind the writing of the text. A document like this must by its nature be brief but this means that the method that lies behind its use of texts remains at best opaque and at worst invisible. Nevertheless, the impression gained from BEM, and supported by Tabbernee,[40] is that the historical critical method is the dominant hermeneutical method that lies behind it. In this, BEM is a child of its time. In 1982, the shift in biblical studies that saw an influx of many different approaches to the interpretation of the Bible was only just beginning. Although this change cannot be attributed to one person alone, many people regard Brevard Childs' book

Biblical Theology in Crisis published in 1970[41] as being the watershed between a predominant acceptance of the historical critical method as the primary mode of biblical interpretation and a much more diverse situation in which a variety of methods are used. Biblical interpretation did not change overnight but, from 1970 onwards, other methods began to be used. John Barton comments that, although in the 1970s and 1980s there seemed to be 'sharp controversies' between biblical scholars in contrast to the 1990s, they were 'really quite placid and conciliatory'. The situation of the 1990s he sees as one of 'turmoil' as regards the extent of variety of methods used and the lack of agreement about which method to use that existed then and continues to do so now.[42]

Modern biblical interpretation is characterized by variety. This manifests itself in two ways. The most noticeable is the fact that different interpretations of the Bible are now commonplace. These different methods are not only interested in the historical reconstruction of the text and the events that lie behind it, as the historical critical method was, but in how meaning is conveyed by the Bible and how the context of the person reading it affects their understanding of its meaning (a helpful survey of this variety can be found in the Roman Catholic document *The Interpretation of the Bible in the Church*).[43] A second indication of the variety that now exists in biblical studies is that even where the historical critical method is still employed, and it remains a vital force in biblical scholarship, there is less and less agreement about its findings. It is increasingly hard to find a consensus of opinion about anything in biblical studies.

BEM, written as it was in the 1980s, appropriately reflected the biblical studies of its time. A document written today could not look like this, as is clear from *A Treasure in Earthen Vessels*. One of the primary themes that come out of *A Treasure in Earthen Vessels* is the diversity of methods that abound in the interpretation of the Bible and the importance of acknowledging the diversity of the contexts of the different readers of the Bible. This acknowledgement of the diversity of biblical interpretation is vital within ecumenical debate but will change the documents that emerge from it.

We noted above that one of the significant aspects of BEM is that it is the first attempt to put into practice the Montreal statement on the Bible and its place in ecumenism. It is not clear how the findings and suggestions of *A Treasure in Earthen Vessels* might find practical expression, though its conclusions have a different status to those of the Montreal statement. The debate about the use of the Bible in ecumenism has always been a challenging one but never more so than now. The aim of ecumenical documents has been to reflect those things that the member communities hold in common. The ever decreasing amount of consensus between biblical scholars about what texts mean or even how they should be interpreted, makes the use of the Bible in ecumenical documents increasingly complex. There is general agreement that the Bible should be used but how it should be used is less clear.

conclusions

BEM's use of the Bible is thorough. The editors of the text have taken great care to weave biblical references and allusions throughout the document to support and illustrate the points that they are making. This attempt is impressive and effective and set a very high standard for the use of the Bible in subsequent ecumenical debate. Nevertheless we have noted all the way through this study that problems emerge in this use of the Bible. These problems need to be acknowledged and addressed in future ecumenical debates and the documents that arise from them.

This conclusion is split into two parts. The first looks at the small issues that can be addressed relatively easily. The second raises a rather more weighty problem which would require a fundamental rethink of the way the Bible is used in ecumenical documents.

small considerations

The most straightforward pitfall to avoid is the *de facto* adoption of a canon within a canon with weighting towards Paul almost at the exclusion of the Old Testament. Ecumenical documents should show in practice that they have their roots in the Old Testament and in the whole of the New Testament. While it is inevitable that Paul's writings will be used extensively this should not be at the expense of other texts. It would be fairly easy to survey the texts used in documents and to confirm that they span the whole canon. Where one text occurs more often than others, as Galatians 3.27-28 did in BEM, other texts which express a similar sentiment might be sought and inserted instead.

Connected to this should be a concern to confirm that references, used to support a point, genuinely do so and that this will be clear to the reader of the text. It is fair to assume biblical literacy on the part of a reader[44] but not that a slightly obscure point can be understood without explanation. This may involve exploring the debates in biblical scholarship about certain disputed texts and to reflect this in the body of the document. For example, when the words of 1 Corinthians 11.23-25 were used to illustrate the institution of the Eucharist[45] the fact that it was the earliest written account could have been reflected briefly in the text with something like: 'St Paul wrote, in what is the earliest account of the institution, "I have received . . .".

larger considerations

Such issues are straightforward to address. Rather more fundamental is the perennial problem of the accusation of prooftexting and the increasing diversity of biblical interpretation. Ecumenical documents will never be free of this accusation until the method of demonstrating roots in the Bible changes. Biblical quotations and citations do not demonstrate that a debate has the Bible as its source. Instead they demonstrate that the Bible has been called in as a witness to support a point already made. This point may have arisen in debate from biblical sources but, as this is not demonstrated, the documents will always be open to the accusation of prooftexting.

A way of avoiding this is to begin documents, and sections of documents, by painting a brief 'biblical picture' on the topic, based in biblical scholarship. This could then form the underpinning for the subsequent discussion of the subject. For example, a section on baptism might begin by sketching out the impact of the symbol of water in the Old Testament, the ritual of cleansing in Judaism (and how baptism differs from that), what baptism was used for and symbolized in John the Baptist's ministry and Jesus' own ministry, how it was taken on in the early Church and what it came to mean to Paul. This would give a biblical foundation to which subsequent discussion could return and expand but would have, in the first place, expressed the variety of uses of baptism in the Bible and an acknowledgement of the issues that arise from this.

In order to express the true diversity of the Bible and its interpretations some examples of differing interpretations from the same biblical texts might need to be given (both from biblical scholarship and different denominations and geographic regions). This would illustrate and acknowledge the depth of diversity that can exist in biblical interpretation before moving towards a more common statement which reflects the unity that arises out of this diversity. Such an approach would be a new departure in such documents and would require detailed biblical work as the foundation for discussion and debate. The advantage of it, however, would be a firm basis within the Bible and the potential to reflect the diversity that exists within it and within biblical scholarship.

It is good that the Bible plays such a significant role within ecumenical debate but it is important that theoretical statements made about this importance are matched in practice and reflected in the most important ecumenical documents. The value of BEM's use of the Bible is that it put into practice the widely accepted Montreal statement. In doing so, it illustrated the difficulty of applying such theory within ecumenical documents. This problem is even greater for the writers of contemporary ecumenical documents than it was for the writers of BEM, as the theory of biblical interpretation gets more and more complex. These difficulties, however, ought not to dissuade people from using the Bible in ecumenical documents but to encourage them into greater vigilance about how they use it.

Writers of ecumenical documents should strive to use texts from as much of the canon of Scripture as possible, aiming not to represent one author or one text more than others. They should seek to ensure that it is clear why a certain text has been used and where relevant to present, in brief, significant scholarly insights into a particular text. They should acknowledge and represent variety in their use of the Bible by recognizing both that the Bible is a varied text speaking with different voices at different times and that the Bible is interpreted variously by its different readers. Most importantly of all, however, writers of ecumenical documents should not assume that it is clear that an ecumenical document is rooted in Scripture simply when it has references to the Bible in it. If writers wish to demonstrate a rooting in Scripture, as full a picture as possible should be drawn from the biblical evidence illustrating its breadth and complexity. Demonstrating that 'we exist as Christians by the Tradition of the gospel . . . testified in scripture'[46] requires a more nuanced use of the Bible than has been evident in the past. BEM was an important staging post on the way but much more work needs to be done if future ecumenical texts are to build on the foundations laid down by BEM.

chapter six

rethinking ecumenical theology

Paul Avis

The ecumenical movement seems to have reached a watershed. Its momentum slowed noticeably in the last decade of the twentieth century. In the first decade of the new century it is definitely faltering. The dreams that marked the heyday of ecumenism, of 'the coming great church' and of visible unity by the year 'whatever', now look naive, if not reckless. Ecumenical endeavour is now shot through with doubt and uncertainty. Inertia and apathy confront ecumenism on every side. A fresh vision is now needed and ecumenical theology needs to be reconstructed. The eschatological hope of the full visible unity of the Body of Christ that has motivated the ecumenical movement for nearly a century is still valid, but the way that this is articulated theologically and practically is changing. This chapter explores two aspects of that changed perception: first the relationship between unity and diversity and second the connection between unity and mission.

Few informed Christians would deny that the ecumenical movement has achieved a great deal – transforming attitudes, promoting understanding, discovering common ground, stimulating cooperation, even facilitating some structural unions. However, the classical vision of visible unity (defined as all Christians in each place in visible unity with all Christians in every place) that was pioneered by the Faith and Order movement and set out by the New Delhi Assembly of the World Council of Churches in 1961 has not been translated into reality, except in a piecemeal and fragmentary way. The goal of the full visible unity of the currently divided Christian Church continues to be affirmed by various Churches, especially by Anglicans and Roman Catholics, but the practical realization of the goal seems to be receding.

On the other hand, the gains that the ecumenical movement has made have been assimilated into church life. Mutual respect, understanding and cooperation between individual Christians and between Christian Churches can now largely be taken for granted.

Many Christians enjoy these benefits, unaware of the struggle and the cost that brought them about. To some Christians unity is simply of the heart. Charity, and with it courtesy, is what matters. 'Spiritual' unity is enough. The momentum of the ecumenical movement is flagging partly because its values have been transposed into church life across the board. I suggest that three specific features of the current ecumenical mood can be discerned.

First, there is a greater realism about the ecclesial identity of the Churches that are active in the ecumenical movement. This mood of realism acknowledges how hard won and how deeply entrenched are the various positions about the nature of the Church held by different Christian traditions. For some (particularly in the Lutheran tradition) the Church's unity is given by God in the ministry of word and sacrament – given dynamically, kerygmatically (i.e. in the action of proclaiming the gospel), in a way that cannot be tied down structurally. Linked very often to this stance is a suspicion of visible, historical structures of oversight that stems from the opposition of the popes and many bishops to the Reformation in the sixteenth century. For others, those in the broadly Catholic tradition, the Christian Church is essentially a visible, structured community or society that continues to have a real existence through time and space. For them, the life of the visible Church has a sacramental quality and structures of ministry and oversight are the channels through which the Holy Spirit normally works. Comparable differences emerge over understandings of authority, ordination, episcopacy and universal primacy.

These differences in the understanding of the Church and of its visibility are not minor or superficial. They reflect different theological worldviews, so to speak. They have to do with the relations between creation and redemption, nature and grace, matter and spirit, and to that extent they shadow the tensions in the Western philosophical tradition since the pre-Socratic philosophers and Plato and Aristotle. Few of us who are professionally engaged in ecumenical dialogue would concede that these theological differences are completely intractable. But ecumenism is increasingly seen as the art of the possible for the basic reason that different ecclesial identities go very deep and need to be taken seriously.

Second, there is an urgency about mission and specifically about evangelism in an increasingly secular and pluralist culture in which the Churches find themselves steadily losing ground in numbers, resources and influence. The true ecumenist knows that unity and mission are inseparable in the purposes of God (the *missio dei*);

that they are two sides of the one coin; that God purposed to unite all things in and through Jesus Christ. But there are some voices in the Churches that do not acknowledge any intrinsic connection between mission and unity and claim that mission can be pursued successfully without being linked to unity. I believe that what they advocate is not the kind of mission that Scripture mandates, that has theological integrity and that glorifies God. Appalling damage has been done to the mission of the gospel by the public divisions and oppositions between Christians. There is a unique power and effectiveness in united witness and shared service. To be credible in today's climate, the cause of unity must be explicitly linked to the cause of mission. The quest for visible unity is not only an end in itself – because it brings to light the true nature of the Church as the indivisible Body of Christ – it is also a means to an end: effective mission and evangelism.

Third, the first two concerns taken together (the reality of ecclesial identity and the imperative of mission) highlight the reality of diversity, of difference, within the broad Christian tradition. As Newman once said, You cannot have Christianity and not have differences. To come up, as we sometimes do in ecumenical dialogue, against the rock of apparently intractable difference prompts much greater realism than has sometimes been the case about the sort of unity that might be desirable and achievable. The urgent demand of mission and evangelism encourages a positive view of Christian diversity as a multi-channelled medium for the gospel. It is this third area, the relation between unity and diversity, that I want to explore more deeply next.

taking diversity seriously

We can get something of a grip on the complex issue of diversity by distinguishing between two aspects: diachronic diversity (diversity across time – historical diversity) and synchronic diversity (diversity across space – contemporary diversity). The plurality of Christian traditions of liturgy, theology and spirituality can be viewed from both angles. The historical and the contemporary interact at every point in time and space. The two dimensions correspond to the last two of the four attributes of the Church that we confess in the 'Nicene' Creed: unity, holiness, catholicity and apostolicity. Apostolicity is primarily diachronic: it refers to the calling of the Church to be faithful to the mission of the Apostles and particularly to the apostolic faith in its own ongoing mission. Catholicity is primarily synchronic: it points to the universal scope of the salvation that is offered to the world through the mission of the Church.

Ecumenical theology is concerned with both diachronic and synchronic diversity in the Church. Diachronic diversity comes into play in the attempt to hear, to understand and to evaluate the different participating traditions: their origins, stories, trajectories and memories. Synchronic diversity becomes operative in the search for a unity that has integrity while embracing diversity and allowing all the partners in the quest to contribute the distinctiveness of their communities.

This interactive process of mutual learning and mutual critique marks ecumenical engagement as profoundly spiritual, relational and personal. It takes place in the mode of 'personal knowledge', not of the dry rational analysis of texts and concepts. It is concerned with the rapport that is created between communities, not with juggling unwieldy institutions and trying to match up asymmetrical structures. It demands the art of listening empathetically and of discerning what is dear to one's ecumenical dialogue partner, the ecumenical 'other'. It calls for the intellectual generosity that is able to recognize the same meaning in different words and the same values in different practices, as well as the intellectual rigour that is willing to name significant differences when they are clearly evident, rather than sweeping them under the carpet.

In the last resort, ecumenical dialogue requires courage to make judgements about our own tradition, when we have made the effort to know it in its integrity, and about the tradition of others, when we have made the effort to understand that in its integrity also. At the end of the day we still have to make crucial theological judgements on which we will not all agree. We have to decide whether unity is visible and structural or not (whatever more it may be); whether episcopacy belongs to the full visible unity of the Church or not; whether a universal primacy is God's will for the Church, or not (and if so, what sort of primacy). In making such judgements, we are not required to play down, to relativize the diversity of the traditions. We are not obliged to pretend *per impossibile* that all forms of being Church are of equal value, that all ecclesiologies stand at an equal distance from God's will for the Church. But what we are called to discern in other Churches, if we can, is their fundamental ecclesial integrity, the reality of the *koinonia* that they enjoy with the Father and the Son and with each other through the Holy Spirit, the authenticity of their ministries of word and sacrament, the vitality of their means of grace. We are called to seek the presence of the one Church of Jesus Christ in each other's particular Churches. It is just this kind of mutual ecclesial recognition that is reflected in the Meissen Agreement, the Fetter Lane and Reuilly Common Statements and in the Anglican–Methodist Covenant.

What role does diversity play in the New Testament itself? What is the significance of the fact that a diversity of interpretations of the gospel is enshrined in the trust deeds of Christianity, the New Testament writings? It is not controversial that the New Testament canon contains a plurality of theologies and that there are some tensions between them (between Paul and James on faith and works and between Hebraic and Hellenistic frameworks in the gospels, for example).[1] A special significance attaches to the fact that there are Four Gospels. This does not undermine the singularity of the one gospel of Christ (for they are each 'the gospel according to' Matthew, Mark, Luke or John). But it does show that the one gospel is embodied in a number of canonical narratives whose theologies cannot be fully harmonized.[2]

We should also take to heart the pronounced diversity of practice in the apostolic and post-apostolic Churches, those closest to 'the Christ event'. Are their differences in credal confession, in liturgy and in church order merely signs of immaturity in the infant Church, teething troubles, that would eventually be overcome by a centrally policed uniformity, once the great councils had taken place? Or does the diversity of the early, undivided Church bear witness to an essential and ineradicable element in the Church's authentic life? What is indisputable is that uniformity was not an apostolic value.

The theme of diversity can be related also to the doctrine of creation. The belief that God's creative power was bound to find fulfilment in all logically compatible possibilities in the world was expressed in the medieval doctrine of divine plenitude.[3] To see the force of this idea we need look no further than human nature itself. Humankind, created in the image and likeness of God, is characterized by a myriad of differences. The image of God is almost infinitely varied. No two human faces, not even those of identical twins, are completely identical. The genetic footprint of an individual is unique. Every human life is a unique total mystery, known very imperfectly to the subject of it and completely only to God. Diversity reflects both the infinite creativity of the triune God and our human experience of 'otherness'.[4]

Jesus Christ himself is presented in Scripture as including in a representative way in his person the diverse plenitude of the intelligent creation. He incorporates (or recapitulates as some early Fathers said) the outworking of God's purpose in creation. Colossians 1.15ff. brings together the particularity of the Incarnation in Jesus Christ, a single, complete person, on the one hand, and the limitless scope of created diversity, on the other: 'He is the image of the invisible God, the firstborn of all creation.' Unity and diversity are 'held together' and cohere, without violence, in him (v. 17). In him the fullness (pleroma) of God was pleased to find a unique home (katoikesai) (v. 19). In this passage fullness and totality are focused, without being diminished, in a single point: in the one who is 'the head', 'the beginning', 'the firstborn' – in the single person on the single cross (vv. 18-20). These reflections suggest that the ultimate eschatological unity that God intends for God's creation is one that is rich, creative and overflowing to a degree greater than we can imagine.

diversity, unity and mission

The Incarnation of the Son of God can be seen in this light as the unique personal fusion of unity and diversity. Jesus Christ unites the universal and the particular, the eternal and the temporal. In the Incarnation God identifies his being and purpose in a unique, definitive way with a very specific, limited, concrete set of finite particulars that comprise the life of a first-century, Jewish, Aramaic-speaking, single, male Nazarene, who worked as a carpenter and died at the age of 33. As Kierkegaard suggested, this is the significance of the Pauline phrase 'the fullness (pleroma) of time'.[5] But this particular event happened for the sake of universal truth, so that the blessings that flowed from the Incarnation might embrace all human kind and be relevant to all types of human experience. The particular Jesus is also the universal Christ. The value of the particular event is communicated through the universalizing power of symbol, and it is through the symbols that we call sacraments that we also participate in that value.

Christian diversity is not only inscribed in the very 'trust deeds' of Christianity, the New Testament, and rooted in the apostolic and post-apostolic Church. It is also inevitably generated by the success of the gospel and the expansion of the Church. Diversity characterizes the human response, inspired by the Holy Spirit, to the unfathomable richness and splendour of the gospel. The fact of diversity signifies that a proper inculturation of the gospel has occurred. Once again we see how diversity belongs to the catholicity of the Church. The Lutheran theologian Harding Meyer suggests that when the idea of catholicity is understood as standing for the universal totality, fullness and integrity of the Church, diversity and difference are seen in a new light. 'They no longer appear as a threat to unity. Rather they can be conceived as essential marks of unity.'[6]

We are familiar with the imperative of unity, expressed classically in the high-priestly prayer of John 17.21: 'May they all be one.' But there is also an imperative of diversity: the Lord prays not only for his Apostles but also for all those who will come to believe in him through their witness (v. 20). They too will be touched with the glory that comes from unity in multiplicity (v. 22). The Johannine post-Resurrection appearance of Jesus by the lakeside, when under his direction the disciples land a catch of 153 large fish, yet without breaking their net, points to the same truth: multiplicity, diversity, held in unbreakable unity (John 21.9ff.). It is, therefore, not only unity but diversity as well that is the ecumenical imperative. The Canberra Assembly of the World Council of Churches (1991) stated:

> Diversities which are rooted in theological traditions, various cultural, ethnic, or historical contacts are integral to the nature of communion . . . In communion diversities are brought together in harmony as gifts of the Holy Spirit, contributing to the richness and fullness of the church of God.

It is the effectiveness of mission, as the gospel is spoken into different cultures and contexts, that is the real source of diversity in the Church. This process is circular and self-perpetuating: diversity of expressions of the gospel is an instrument of mission, corresponding to the diversity of cultures. Diversity creates a multiplicity of access points for evangelization. Therefore, just as mission creates diversity, it also demands unity, so that the diversity remains rooted in the one gospel. This suggests that ecumenism is a response to the success of mission. Mission is the origin of diversity.[7]

diversity, relativism and truth

The sheer fact of diversity, quite apart from the various ways in which it might be evaluated, points up the role of human history and culture in shaping the Church's belief and practice. 'The Church's life and work are shaped by its historical origins, by its subsequent experience, and by its endeavour to make the relevance of the gospel plain to every generation.'[8] Once again, diversity is seen as an aspect of the catholicity of the gospel. But this insight has subversive implications. The catholicity of the gospel implies that the Christian faith is greater than any particular individual, community or historical period is capable of grasping.

At the same time, however, the dimension of apostolicity provides the vital element of continuity, of essential identity. Catholicity and diversity are balanced by apostolicity and coherence. The tension between the discontinuity of diversity and the continuity of the apostolic mission ensures that the transcendence, the sovereignty of the gospel is upheld. We never have God's word under our control or within our grasp. We may have stewardship, never possession. The gospel is not free-floating – it is always embodied – but it remains free under the sway of the Spirit (John 3.8).

When we acknowledge diversity in the expression of Christian faith, we thereby relativize our own standpoint. We cannot make absolute claims for our particular grasp of the truth while at the same time recognizing that other interpretations have authenticity. The truth stands beyond any individual's grasp of it. No one can hold the truth in the palm of their hand.[9]

However, to acknowledge diversity in principle, while it has the effect of relativizing our own grasp of truth, does not relativize the Truth itself. Truth subsists in God. Ultimately the truth is identical with God. Jesus Christ is the definitive revelation of the truth of God in so far as that can be compressed into a single, short human life: 'I am the Way, the Truth and the Life' (John 14.6). It is only our human responses to the Truth that are relativized – our failure to walk the Way and to live the Life that are Christ.

This is not philosophical scepticism. That school of thought either questions whether there is an ultimate truth at all (radical scepticism); or, if the existence of truth is not challenged, doubts the human possibility of apprehending it to any meaningful extent (radical agnosticism). At any rate, it holds that systems of belief and value cannot ultimately be judged one against another. In Isaiah Berlin's idiom, belief and value systems are incommensurable. That is very different to the cognitive humility that has characterized the apophatic (via negativa) tradition within Christianity. The Cloud of Unknowing spoke of the God who could be loved but not known, loved with the heart but not known with the head.[10] The apophatic tradition (the tradition of negative theology, of proceeding by stating what God is not) implies that there is much that we cannot see clearly, much that we can never know, a vast hinterland of mystery.

A realist approach to diversity is one that takes difference to be (at least sometimes) cognitive, not just expressive, that is to say, the difference is in our thinking, not just in the way we state it. It is not that various Christian traditions and theologies are all saying the same thing in different words and idioms, but that they are actually saying some different things (as well, of course, as some very important things on which they speak with one voice). Ecumenical work jumps too readily to the conclusion that differences are only semantic. To attribute oppositions in Christianity simply to differences of perspective or terminology is an attractive option that ecumenical dialogue has sometimes fallen for. However, a tough ecumenical theology will be alert to instances of real cognitive difference and will not allow sentiment or pragmatism to gloss over them.[11]

A serious acknowledgement of diversity has significant implications for the exercise of authority in the Church. It undermines the Church's ability to take decisions in the realms of belief and practice that are intended to be the final word. (Certainly it rules out any claim to put an end to discussion, as has sometimes been tried.) Such statements cannot be definitive because they cannot be universal: that is to say, they cannot transcend their particular historical and cultural contexts. Even within one Church different theological traditions and schools of thought find it difficult to understand each other and to hold dialogue because they are operating on somewhat different premises.[12] There is a plurality of human responses to divine revelation. None of these responses, given the reality of pluralism, can be claimed to be the last word. If one tradition of response is privileged in this way, the validity of diversity, as an aspect of theological method, is undermined. You cannot impose uniformity of interpretation at the same time as you affirm the authenticity of diverse ways of being a Christian in the Church.

Recognition of diversity, therefore, removes the possibility of demonstrable certainty in the area of belief. No absolute, objective certainty can be predicated of any set of beliefs. This sentiment chimes in with the classic Anglican doctrine of probability that runs right through the centuries: from Hooker through the early Liberal Anglicans and Locke, to Joseph Butler, Burke, Keble and Gladstone, right up to A. E. Taylor and most recently Basil Mitchell. To take diversity seriously enhances the importance of probability as 'the guide to life' (Butler) and to that extent is amenable to the Anglican approach to theology which is practical and pastoral rather than speculative and dogmatic. 'We live by faith, not by sight' (2 Corinthians 5.7). Faith brings its own assurance, its own conviction (Hebrews 11.1; 6.11). This is enough to walk by in daily discipleship and gives a firm ground for hope. But it is not a basis for irreformable theological statements, binding on the conscience – as if to say: 'You must believe in this way and this way only, or you cannot belong.'

how much diversity is compatible with unity?

The question of the mutual compatibility of unity and diversity can be posed either way round. In the past ecumenical theology has tended to ask: How much diversity is compatible with unity? But today we are more likely to ask: What sort of unity is compatible with diversity? In their internal discussions Churches and world communions wrestle with the question of the limits to diversity. How can diversity be affirmed without imperilling communion?

The Fetter Lane Common Statement by the Church of England and the Moravian Church offers a case study in communion and diversity. Chapter VI (paragraphs 50 and 51) contains a vision of visible unity that would not involve a loss of identity on the part of either partner. It stresses that the distinctive ethos of both traditions to a partnership should be nurtured and shared within visible unity in a number of key areas: spirituality, liturgy, hymnody, ways of doing theology, ways of being Christian community, styles of oversight and episcopacy, styles of mission, ways of honouring the memories of our histories, commemoration of our saints, martyrs and of memorial days, links with global structures of fellowship, the honouring of other ecumenical partnerships. It claims that this approach to communion with diversity has considerable ecumenical significance and could provide a model for a more inclusive united Church in England. It should reassure those who fear that making a commitment to visible unity might lead to a monolithic organizational structure. The guiding principle is that the unity that we seek with others cannot be less diverse than the comprehensiveness that is already found in each of our Churches.[13]

If diversity is related to the apostolicity and catholicity of the Church, it cannot be unexamined, uncritical diversity. Not all cultural forms of Christianity will be equally authentic. They need to be loyal to apostolic faith and order as grounded in the New Testament and interpreted by the ecumenical creeds. Diversity cannot be unconditionally celebrated. When, in a hackneyed expression, ecclesiological texts invoke 'rich diversity', we have learned to suspect that the argument has dried up.

The appeal to diversity always needs to be qualified. The qualifiers most commonly found in ecclesial texts (apart from 'rich'!) are 'legitimate', 'tolerable' or 'salutary'. Vatican II speaks of 'lawful diversity', which seems to imply a strong role for the Magisterium in deciding and enforcing what diversity will be allowed. But Vatican II also helpfully emphasizes that the bonds that unite the faithful are stronger than what divides them.[14] Pope John Paul II speaks of 'unity in legitimate diversity' in *Ut Unum Sint*.[15] This rather suggests that, while there may be acceptable forms of diversity in the Church, there will nevertheless remain a unitary Magisterium that decides what expressions of diversity are legitimate.

One principle to get clear is that diversity is not opposed to unity. The opposite of unity is not diversity but division. The opposite of diversity is not unity but uniformity. If we set our face against division, on the one hand, and uniformity on the other, we should find ourselves steering a course towards communion in diversity.

unity and mission: towards integration

The mission agenda and the ecumenical agenda of the Churches are sometimes seen as alternative priorities, in the sense that you might have to choose between them. They are regarded as discrete activities that can be carried on separately, rather than as mutually dependent aspects of the one task of the Church. The indissoluble biblical and theological connection between them is not always appreciated. Putting unity and mission into separate compartments like that implies a deficient theology of both mission and unity.

In the first place it involves a seriously inadequate view of mission – one that leaves the nature of the Church out of account and fails to grasp that mission is an ecclesiological matter. It tends to assume that mission is simply a matter of individuals evangelising individuals and not also a witness of communities to communities and of a society to societies. The communities that are engaged in mission are the local churches (i.e. dioceses), made up of parishes that are themselves Church, engaging with the communities in which they are embedded. The society that engages in mission is the Church in its ordered life, with its structures of ministry and oversight. It relates as an institution to the institutions of civil society. When mission is radically individualized, however, its ecclesial nature becomes eclipsed.

Mission is a holistic activity. To anticipate some work that I am doing in another connection, it is 'the whole Church bringing the whole Christ to the whole world'. Its essence is given in the threefold mandate of the risen Christ to the Apostles in the Great Commission (Matthew 28.18-20): to make disciples, to administer baptism and to teach all that Jesus had commanded. With only a little theological licence, this threefold task can be seen to correspond to the salient themes in the Church of England's ordinals (the ordinal appended to the 1662 *Book of Common Prayer* and the one included in *The Alternative Service Book 1980*). These themes are the ministry of the word (proclaiming the gospel and teaching the faith), the administration of the sacraments of baptism and the Eucharist, and the exercise of pastoral care and oversight. In turn, they relate to the threefold nature of the Church as the body of Christ: prophetic, priestly and royal. And this in turn reflects the threefold messianic identity of Jesus Christ, our great Prophet, Priest and King.

Mission is a task given to the Church for the sake of the world (Mark 16.15; John 3.16). A mission to the world as a whole can only be carried out by the Church as a whole. Mission is a profoundly ecclesial activity. As the mission entrusted to the Church as such, it demands united witness, shared service and the visible demonstration of 'the unity of the Spirit in the bond of peace' (Ephesians 4.3).

By the same token, unity has sometimes had its own separate agenda. It has been thought to require a distinct set of 'ecumenical' activities, mostly additional interchurch meetings, that it is not easy to identify with the 'core activities' of the Church of Christ – worship, proclamation and evangelism. Tinged as it often is with sentimentality and pragmatism, ecumenism has lost credibility among those seized by the urgency of mission. Unity is not about doing extra ecumenical things, things that absorb precious time and energy, but about doing the things we should be doing anyway *ecumenically*: worshipping, witnessing, serving and evangelizing *as one* and so releasing energy rather than absorbing it.

This dualistic thinking about unity and mission needs to be superseded by a holistic, integrated approach that sees how they are bound together in the purposes of God. The report of the Anglican–Reformed International Commission, *God's Reign and Our Unity* (1984), noted that often the concern for evangelism, social justice and church unity are set against each other. Its response was to affirm that 'the Father . . . sent his Son to preach the gospel, to proclaim justice for the oppressed and to draw together all his disciples into the unity of the Godhead'. Therefore, evangelism, social justice and church unity 'are not conflicting concerns, but are complementary aspects of the one mission of God'.[16]

In the life of the Church a passionate concern for mission has led to an enhanced concern for unity. Conversely, when the imperative of unity is taken seriously, it is usually bound up with a commitment to mission. This logic makes sense: when the Church stands out from the world in a heightened concern for mission, the differences between the Churches sink into the background and what they have in common becomes more prominent.

For nearly a century, mission and unity have been intimately linked in ecumenism. It was when the modern missionary movement was at its peak, at the turn of the nineteenth century, and when John R. Mott's slogan 'The evangelization of the world in this generation' was coming into vogue, that the conscience of Christians involved in mission began to be deeply troubled by the divisions within the Church. It was borne in upon Christian leaders that, while the Churches were competing with one another and sometimes in a state of outright opposition, the credibility of the gospel was undermined, not least on the mission field, but also at home, and Christ was dishonoured.

The International Missionary Conference at Edinburgh in 1910 brought together for the first time, on a world scale, the twin concerns of mission and unity and demonstrated their connection. However, the conference discovered by experience that mission and unity could not be held together if questions of doctrine and church order were excluded, as they had necessarily been in order to persuade Christian leaders of different persuasions to talk to each other. The unfinished ecclesiological business of Edinburgh 1910 was continued at the first world Faith and Order Conference at Lausanne in 1927, while mission concerns were channelled through the International Missionary Council (IMC). The IMC became part of the World Council of Churches in 1961, which already included Faith and Order and Life and Work. In the WCC unity and mission were united organizationally.

Writing about these developments in 1954, Bishop G. K. A. Bell stressed the indissoluble connection between mission and unity. He quoted Charles Ranson of the IMC:

> Wherever the Church recognises itself as standing in a missionary situation, the question of unity becomes vital.

The complacency of the Churches concerning their disunity can only be accounted for by the loss of the conviction that the Church exists to fulfil a mission.

It was no accident, Ranson pointed out, that the foundations of the modern ecumenical movement, with its concern for Christian unity, were laid by the missionary movement.[17]

If space allowed we could trace the connection between mission and unity through a number of ecumenical and ecclesiological developments during the past century, from the Lambeth Conference Appeal to All Christian People of 1920 to the documents of the Second Vatican Council. Anglican–Methodist dialogue is particularly strong on the connection between unity and mission and it runs like a golden thread through the Anglican–Methodist Covenant.

Modern missiology is permeated by the idea of the *missio dei*: it is beginning to infuse ecumenical theology also. The concept, if not the term, originated with Karl Barth in the early 1930s. Barth began to speak of mission as an activity of God. At the Willingen conference of the International Missionary Council (part of the World Council of Churches) in 1952, mission was explicitly seen as deriving from the very nature of God and was interpreted in the light of the doctrine of the Holy Trinity. According to this insight, Father, Son and Holy Spirit, three Persons in one God, send the Church into the world. The Church exists because God's mission is under way.

In his exposition of the theology of the New Testament, Alan Richardson wrote:

> Church unity is not a 'desirable feature' in the life of the Church; it is the condition of the Church's existence, the test of whether the Church is the Church. A divided Church is a contradiction of its own nature as Church; it is witnessing to a falsehood. Its evangelism cannot be effective . . . If we took the New Testament point of view seriously, we should expect to find that the single most serious obstacle to the evangelization of the world is the disunity of 'the churches'.[18]

sending and gathering

Unity and mission are bound together in God's undivided purpose to reconcile all things through Christ. This grand theme that runs through Scripture can be construed under the rubric of sending and gathering. These two verbs encompass the divine salvific action in the world – the *missio dei*. God is at work in the world, expressing his gracious purpose in this twofold way. This divine action is the action of the triune God. According to the wisdom of the early Fathers, the action of God *ad extra* is the action of the three Persons of the Holy Trinity acting indivisibly, so to speak.

There is a triune action in sending. The Father sends the Son into the world out of love for the world. The Father and the Son together send the Holy Spirit upon the Church to empower its mission. Jesus sends the Apostles into the world on behalf of the Father, at the same time enduing them with the Holy Spirit (John 3.16; 8.18, 29,42; 17.18; 14.16,26; 15.26; 16.7; 20.21; Matthew 28.19; Luke 24.49).

There is also a triune action in gathering. The gracious purpose of 'the God and Father of our Lord Jesus Christ', that he 'set forth' in the coming of Jesus Christ, was 'to gather up all things in him, things in heaven and things on earth'. The pledge that this purpose will ultimately be completed is the seal of the Holy Spirit that already marks believers (Ephesians 1.3-14). Against the background of triune divine action, the point is being made that he was *sent* to *gather*.

In St John's Gospel, Jesus foretells that when he is lifted up he will draw all people to himself, gathering them at the cross (John 12.32). St John pointedly states that Caiaphas, the High Priest, prophesied unwittingly 'that Jesus was about to die for the nation, and not for the nation only, but to gather into one the dispersed children of God' (John 11.51-52). There seems to be a deliberate echo here of the scattering of the peoples in judgement at the fall of the Tower of Babel (Genesis 11.8-9) and the promise to Abraham, that almost immediately follows in Genesis, that in him and his descendants all the families of the earth would be blessed (Genesis 12.2-3). In the Old Testament prophets, the promise that God will gather from among the nations his scattered people, and indeed gather the nations themselves together on Mount Zion (Jerusalem) is extensively developed (Isaiah 43.5-6; 49.5-6; 60.1-16; Ezekiel 37.21; 39.27, etc.).

The Old Testament imagery of YHWH as the Shepherd of his people, gathering the scattered sheep into the fold of their own land (Ezekiel 34), is also echoed in St John. The Good Shepherd gathers the sheep, scattered by the wolf, into one fold by laying down his life in order that he might take it up again (John 10.11-18). Thus his redeemed people are gathered into the fold of the Church at the cross. But they can only be united in the power of his risen life. That life springs out of the cross. It is the cross on which Christ is glorified (John 17.1-5). The cross is planted in a garden, like the Tree of Life in Eden (John 19.41). It is as he displays his wounds to them that the risen Lord breathes the Holy Spirit upon them and sends them forth (John 20.19-23). St Paul also identifies the power of the resurrection with the Holy Spirit (Romans 1.4; 1 Timothy 3.16). It is the Holy Spirit who enables baptized believers to enter into the reality of unity.

Once you ground the sending of the Church in the triune nature of God, you infuse the idea of mission with the idea of unity. They can no longer be held in separation. You cannot speak of the one without the other. The one God cannot generate a mission that is fragmented and divided. Conversely, the life of the Church, the face it shows to the world, must faithfully reflect the dynamic unity of the God who has sent it. The two interconnected movements of the *missio dei* are sending and gathering, mission and unity. The movement of sending out into the world is for the sake of gathering into the kingdom. Neither sending nor gathering can happen without the other. The relatedness and the tension between them are grounded in the Trinitarian action of God which embraces both these movements. The action of God in the world must lead to unity for the simple reason that it flows from unity.

chapter seven

seeking the one, holy, catholic and apostolic Church: do bishops exhibit or obscure it?

Christopher Hill

full, visible unity: an ambiguous goal?

As one reads these essays a particular issue emerges with some clarity. While recognizing a difference of emphasis between the various ecumenical statements, Peter Fisher (Chapter 2) notes an increasing tendency to affirm a visible unity in diversity on the basis of an ecclesiology of *koinonia* (or communion) grounded in the doctrine of the Holy Trinity. He emphasizes the consistently stated goal of visible unity in all recent Anglican dialogues with the other Churches and that 'diversity has never been seen as legitimating a less ambitious goal'. Paul Avis (Chapter 6) articulates two emergent basic axioms of visible unity: diversity is inescapable and mission is imperative. Martin Davie (Chapter 3) shows us that while 'official' Anglican organs have consistently been committed to organic unity or full, visible unity, there have been (and remain) at least some Anglican voices who concur with Martin Luther's teaching about the unity of the invisible Church, or who would want to articulate a more nuanced understanding of the relation between the visible and invisible Church as expressed, for example, in the Westminster Confession. Others still have a pietistic understanding of 'spiritual' unity. Peter Fisher speaks ominously of the danger of some forms of expression becoming normative by repetition within ecumenical circles 'whilst remaining obscure or unconvincing outside them'; with consequent danger to a process of genuine reception and abandonment of theological exploration. Is there a danger of the (official) Anglican insistence on 'full, visible unity' becoming such a mantra? Paul Avis also reminds us of a certain ecumenical malaise: the ecumenical movement has reached a watershed in its fortunes, its momentum has slowed, the realization of the goal seems to have become more remote.

At first reading Joy Tetley's consideration of the place of Scripture in our ecumenical conversations (Chapter 4) indicates a rather different set of concerns. Yet running through her chapter there are the three intertwined threads of context, community and reception. Her essay is about the *ecclesial* use (or abuse) of Scripture. In a similar way, Paula Gooder's paper raises questions about the ecumenical use of Scripture in the agreed texts Baptism, Eucharist and Ministry of the Faith and Order Commission of the World Council of Churches. There is no one universally accepted method of interpreting Scripture; and accordingly less likelihood of Scripture offering individuals the 'plain meaning' some still look for. Once again we are inevitably faced with the question of the role of community (the Church) in receiving and interpreting the Scriptures. But in an ecumenical context questions arise: *which* church; how do we *recognize* authentic church; and what part do the Scriptures play in such recognition; are the Scriptures sufficient in themselves for this task or is (for example) a ministry of oversight also required to guide our hermeneutics? Once such questions are raised we are not far from the ecclesiological concerns addressed in the other chapters and the suggestion that the goal of unity is still remote.

John Webster's interrogatory chapter (Chapter 1) invites us to scrutinize the accepted Anglican goal from a dogmatic perspective and to reflect on its ecclesiological basis. In particular, he asks Anglicans to reflect on the special nature of the visibility of the Church. He sums up the matter pithily: 'our account of the goal of ecumenism is only as good as the account of the Church's visibility which undergirds it'. To this he relates a certain unease at the almost exclusive reliance on an ecclesiology of *koinonia* in recent ecumenical texts. He suggests that such ecclesiologies leave less room for a proper distancing between God and the Church than, for example, the ecclesiologies based on the Word,[1] that are somewhat more familiar and congenial to our Evangelical Christian partners. There is surely wisdom in looking again at the ecclesiological foundations of our ecumenical agreements. Not necessarily with a view to starting afresh, but with a view to deepening them and where necessary complementing them and correcting them. I do not necessarily share John Webster's reticence about *koinonia* ecclesiologies: but I do agree that as expressed in some of our ecumenical texts they may need development and correlation to other ways of understanding the Church, especially in relation to soteriology. I would argue for a deepening of *koinonia* ecclesiology rather than its rejection.

The most sustained recent exploration of a *koinonia* ecclesiology from a Protestant *and* ecumenical perspective must be Miroslav Volf's *After Our Likeness: The Church as the Image of the Trinity*.[2] Though Volf argues for a systematic and sustained *koinonia* ecclesiology, he, too, suggests that what sometimes passes for communion ecclesiology can be thin:

> Today, the thesis that ecclesial communion should correspond to trinitarian communion enjoys the status of an almost self-evident proposition. Yet it is surprising that no one has carefully examined just where such correspondences are to be found, nor expended much effort on determining where ecclesial communion reaches the limits of its capacity for such analogy. The result is that reconstructions of these correspondences often say nothing more than the platitude that unity cannot exist without multiplicity not multiplicity without unity, or they demand of human beings in the church the (allegedly) completely selfless love of God. The former is so vague that no one cares to dispute it, and the latter so divine that no one can live it.[3]

Volf himself consciously begins from the insights of Jürgen Moltmann's *The Trinity and the Kingdom: The Doctrine of God*.[4]

The first two parts of Volf's important study next engage sympathetically yet critically with the communion ecclesiologies of (the Catholic) Cardinal Joseph Ratzinger and (the Orthodox) Metropolitan John Zizioulas. Only then does he expound a distinctly Evangelical (Free Church) ecclesiology of *koinonia*: a 'Protestant trinitarian construction of the community of "free and equal" persons' – to quote Moltmann on Volf.

In view of Volf's major contribution to such communion ecclesiology, it is surprising that there has been so little Anglican engagement with his work thus far. This essay attempts to encourage such engagement and to identify ecumenical aspects of Volf's study that bear on current inertia.

koinonia and visibility

For such encouragement it will be helpful first of all to recall the genesis of the relevant ecumenical texts. This cannot be done here in any detail but a full study would show that communion ecclesiologies first developed in Roman Catholic and Orthodox thinking about the local, diocesan, eucharistic church as the full embodiment of the *one* Church yet linked in communion with other such local churches. This was in conscious opposition to a pre-Vatican II structuralist understanding of a 'perfect' or 'complete' society, a single universal Church comprising of mere local departments. How such horizontal ecclesial *koinonia* relates to the communion of the persons in the Holy Trinity in the Roman Catholic and Orthodox traditions is a major part of Volf's ecclesiological exploration. Anglicans have used such a communion ecclesiology for similar reasons in our dialogue with the Roman Catholic Church,[5] recognizing that it secures a proper foundation for a diocesan-based church (as opposed to a single, centralized papal Church with a Universal Bishop) and also for the linkage *between* Churches, through bishops in collegial communion and forms of conciliarity. Nor is it accidental that internal Anglican ecclesiology has also ploughed this furrow, as we do after all call ourselves an Anglican Communion. *The Virginia Report*[6] extensively explores an ecclesiology of communion on an analogy of the *koinonia* of the Trinity. The Inter-Anglican Doctrinal Commission drafted *The Virginia Report* against the background of division within the Anglican Communion on the ordination of women and debate about human sexuality. What should relationships between autonomous provinces be; what space for dissent; what grounds for legitimate intervention; what role for bishops as signs of unity within a diocese and between dioceses; what of other instruments of unity such as the Lambeth Conference and the Archbishop of Canterbury? What, in other words, is the nature of the *koinonia* of the Churches of the Anglican Communion?

One of the most significant examples of a communion ecclesiology in an Anglican–Protestant text is in the Meissen Agreement between the Church of England and the (then two) German Evangelical Churches.[7] A careful reading of the Meissen text, however, reveals an awareness of the dangers of a bland understanding of *koinonia*. In its treatment of the Church as a sign of the kingdom, Meissen recognizes that the Church also shares in the ambiguity and frailty of the human condition and is always in need of repentance, reform and renewal.[8] *Koinonia* is also understood as a share in the sufferings and struggles of humankind in a world alienated from God and divided by disobedience.[9]

Meissen therefore has resonances with other ecclesiologies in which the dynamic of God's will and call, human sin and disobedience, repentance and forgiveness are to the fore. Such textual juxtaposition illustrates both the need and a model for continuing ecclesiological dialogue and an attempt at the balance called for by John Webster.

More unveiling of the history of texts will further open up the issues. As has been shown in these essays, there is a clear family tree to be discerned in the recent ecumenical statements and agreements under discussion: in particular Meissen, Porvoo, Fetter Lane and Reuilly. This can easily be discerned by textual comparison or conjectured more subtly by comparison of members, consultants, observers and staff. This has made for consistency between dialogues; it can, however, obscure development. Reuilly, though chronologically the last, stands in a 'developed' relationship to the earlier texts. The partners involved were the Lutheran and Reformed Churches in France and the Anglican Churches in Britain and Ireland, with observers from the United Reformed Church and the Roman Catholic Church. At a late stage in the work with our French partners, when the basic text was almost complete, an important discussion began on the precise meaning of full, visible unity. The discussion continued after the completion of the text in relation to translation because most of the working text had been drafted in English. Translation of a text requires knowledge of the meaning of the original. So what did 'full, visible unity' mean? André Birmelé – who has given some thought to questions of the visibility of the Church – and I spent the best part of an afternoon on the telephone between Staffordshire and Strasbourg discussing the question as we finalized the translation of the phrase. Put concisely, how do the two adjectives 'full' and 'visible' relate to the noun 'unity'? Does the whole become an adjectival noun? Is the phrase to be construed so that 'full' has the *visibility* of the Church as its referent *rather* than its unity? That there has been no canonized ecumenical interpretation might be deduced from the fact that the English texts show some variation. Meissen speaks of full, visible unity and *volle, sichtbare Einheit*. Porvoo actually avoids the term, speaking simply of visible unity and closer unity. Reuilly avoids the comma and is rendered in French as *la pleine unité visible* – an unusual but legitimate French construction. These highly nuanced linguistic developments reflect the two poles of Anglican ecumenical aspiration: the recognition that there is an already existing visible unity but that this unity still lacks something of the fullness and the increased visibility which the episcopate signals. This bipolar understanding is also reflected in the Anglican commitment to unity by stages.

As Paul Avis has noted, 'unity by stages' has become an axiomatic Anglican principle, in *correlation* with the principle of 'full, visible unity'. The principle is found in the two stages of the first Anglican–Methodist Unity Scheme, the term itself was first employed in the early stages of Anglican–Roman Catholic dialogue.[10] It has a very specific function in the Meissen, Reuilly and the present Anglican–Methodist texts. On the Anglican side there is the formal ecclesial desire to acknowledge the other partners as authentically Church. This clearly entails a real acknowledgement of *unity*, for the Church being acknowledged as such is said to truly participate in the *one*, holy catholic and apostolic Church. Moreover, acknowledgement entails that we know this because we have *seen* it in the partner Church; unity must in some sense be visible for us to be able to recognize it.[11] But Anglicans are also wanting to say that their deepest intuition is that this unity is not as 'full' as it should be because it lacks something more of that visibility Christ intends for his Church as a historical, global, *catholic* community. So, for Anglicans, there is a second stage. John Webster is correct in his hint that at this point in the argument 'the qualifier *full* . . . refers to non-negotiable commitments to a certain understanding of the ministry of oversight'; in other words, bishops in the historic succession and some form of collegial or conciliar connectedness between the Churches. Do we therefore have different theologies of visibility? Is what we already see sufficient for unity, or should we anticipate something more?

visibility and unity

The answer may be a Delphic 'Yes' and 'No'. There is a certain basis for a common understanding of visibility because Anglicans, Lutherans and Reformed have a partially shared confessional history. In answer to the question how we recognize one true Church, *Confessio Augustana* says unambiguously:

> Est enim ecclesia congregatio sanctorum, in qua evangelium recte docetur, et recte administrantur sacramenta. Et ad veram unitatem ecclesiae satis est consentire de doctrina evangelii et administratione sacramentorum.[12]

> The one church of the congregation of the saints is that in which there is a right doctrine of the Gospel and right administration of the sacraments. And for true church unity it is sufficient to agree on the doctrine of the Gospel and the administration of the sacraments.

The Thirty-Nine Articles of Religion of the Church of England speak in similar, though significantly not identical, terms:

> The visible Church of Christ is a congregation of faithful men, in the which the pure Word of God is preached, and the Sacraments be duly administered according to Christ's ordinance in all those things that of necessity are requisite to the same.

Later, Calvin was to write in a more nuanced way (perhaps reflecting his preference for 'Platonic' philosophy) of the Church as known because it is seen:

> Hence the form of the Church appears and stands forth to our view. Wherever we see the Word of God sincerely preached and heard, wherever we see the sacraments administered according to the institution of Christ, there we cannot doubt that the Church of God has some existence, since His promise cannot fail, 'Where two or three are gathered together in my name, there am I in the midst of them' (Matt. 18.20).[13]

The Anglican Articles are less clear on the relationship between the visible and invisible Church than Calvin or the later Reformed tradition, as Oliver O'Donovan has shown in a comparison between Article XIX and Chapter XXV of the Westminster Confession.[14] What is significant for this discussion, however, is that although the Article virtually quotes *Augustana VII* there is no equivalent in the Articles to the important sentence: 'For true church unity *it is sufficient* to agree on the teaching of the Gospel and the administration of the sacraments' (emphasis mine), though there is therefore confessional consensus that the Church is constituted and sustained by Word and Sacrament (and I would add that this is a wider general ecumenical consensus).[15] Augsburg also teaches that this acknowledgement is *sufficient* for unity. To put the matter directly, our Lutheran and Reformed partners are perplexed as to why Anglicans feel obliged to go beyond Word and Sacrament with what for them seems to be the 'addition' of the episcopate. More than this, they have dogmatic reasons for mistrusting Anglican insistence on a wider ministry of oversight as an expression of or condition for 'fuller' unity. It is important for Anglicans to hear such hesitations and objections.

unity and catholicity

We are agreed – the 'we' here are our historic confessions as well as contemporary ecumenical consensus – that the visible Church is constituted and thus recognizable in a communion of Word and

Sacrament. In concrete terms this means at least that wherever an assembly of baptized Christians comes together in praise and penitence; proclaiming and receiving the Word of God and professing their faith; interceding for and being at peace with one another; thanking God for all his gifts in creation and especially for salvation in Christ through the Spirit by sharing the same eucharistic bread and cup; and finally going out in loving service and witness to the world: *here* the *one* Church of Jesus Christ can be seen and known. But *once* having said this, it is difficult to imagine how the experience of unity in Christ through the Spirit in such an evangelical and sacramental community could be further enhanced: how could such a unity and communion be fuller or made more visible than the concrete evangelical and eucharistic assembly? The same truth is enunciated in the Catholic and Orthodox conviction that the whole Church of Christ, and the whole Christ, is fully present in each local eucharistic assembly: the one Church of Christ fully present in each local church. Put somewhat pietistically, what greater degree of unity with God and the congregation could the evangelical imagine than when the Word has been truly spoken, the Supper shared and Christian hearts warmed by the Spirit; or what more could the Catholic aspire to as the eucharistic community kneels adoringly to receive the sacrament in order (in Augustine's phrase) to become what it is, the Body of Christ? What deeper unity with God and the Church, what higher communion with Christ in the Spirit than this? What *greater quality* of unity and visibility could there be?

Anglicans should reverently desire to say 'Amen' to all this, for this also is *our* experience by faith in the power of the Spirit of Christ. Yet, and there must be a yet, Anglicans will want to invite our partners to ponder upon the question of how such a congregation of the Word and Sacrament, how such a faithful eucharistic assembly manifests and expresses its unity and communion with *other such Christian communities*. How is the *communion of the Churches* expressed in both space and in time: how is *synchronic* and *diachronic* catholicity exhibited? But in saying 'yet', Anglicans have the duty to ponder more deeply upon the nature of this wider communion of local churches and how it differs from the visible unity of a given eucharistic community. However, before we explore this further, we must also pay attention to a major problem that stands in the way of the ecclesiological discussion of catholicity I would wish to encourage. John Webster has highlighted the question already: the place of the Church in the economy of salvation. Or put more sharply what, if any, 'mediatorial' role does the Church 'possess'? Unless we attend to this first, no amount of advocacy for episcopacy on the grounds of catholicity will avail. Until this ground is cleared talk of bishops will certainly obscure rather than exhibit the unity and catholicity of the Church.

Christ through the Church?

The Meissen Theological Conference has been the context for theological engagement between the Church of England and the German Protestant Churches, and now includes French Protestant participation. Our partners in these conversations hear that though we acknowledge them as members of an authentic Church this is not yet a sufficient basis for the kind of unity Anglicans believe Christ intends for his one Church, that is to say a wider network of connection, oversight and communion that includes the 'historic' episcopate. In hearing this, our Protestant partners, speaking from their Reformation traditions, begin to interrogate our theology of Church. Yet Anglican apology for the 'historic' episcopate in the last half-century has been largely based on historical grounds. Apart from the difficulty of achieving historic proof[16] our interlocutors put to us a more fundamental question: what weight does history, and the 'historic' episcopate in particular, have ecclesiologically? Surely the only necessary forms of the Church are those given by God? Are Anglicans in danger of making a historically contingent, human structure an ecclesiological necessity? Anglicans feel that such a line of argument begs a number of questions. Does not God work in the history of the Church and the shape of its ministry? Can we divide the Church so rigidly into what is of God and what is of 'merely' human origin? What of the Spirit directing the Church? What of the Church as the Body of Christ; what of being 'in' Christ and Christ being united to us 'head and members'? What of the Church as the continuing community of Jesus the Word-made-flesh, the Word made flesh in human history? Such a sketch of our conversations is, of course, in some danger of caricature, nevertheless I think there are enough brush-strokes for recognition.

At this point our evangelical partners begin to ask whether we are not introducing the notion of a structure in the Church or the Church itself as representing Christ, a 'sacrament' of Christ. Here is Ingolf Dalferth expressing this unease with some clarity: 'Behind *Porvoo's* theology of sign lie elements of an undeclared and unelaborated *sacramental theology . . . a sacramental understanding of ordination to the ministry of the Church* and of *consecration to the episcopate office . . .'* (original emphasis).[17]

He also understands the Anglican defence of episcopacy to entail a soteriological claim: 'although it does not guarantee the presence of the apostolic tradition, and thereby the valid and effective mediation of salvation . . . [it] certainly symbolizes it visibly'.[18]

Engagement with these questions will involve a rather more vigorous application to ecclesiology than we have attempted thus far, either denominationally or ecumenically. There are, however, some building blocks available. Some of the ecumenical dialogues have begun an exploration of the sacramentality of the Church, whether or not such technical 'catholic' language has been used. Such an approach is not only to be found, as might be expected, in Anglican–Roman Catholic dialogue,[19] but perhaps more surprisingly it is first found in the Anglican–Reformed text, *God's Reign and Our Unity*: 'The Church is sent into the world as a sign, instrument and first-fruits of a reality which comes from beyond history – the Kingdom, or reign of God.'[20]

There is also the beginning of discussion also related to the visibility of the Church, of a distinction between the 'foundation' of the Church and its 'shape'. This has taken place within the Leuenberg Church Fellowship in their ecclesiological text, *The Church of Jesus Christ*.[21] Significantly, it is agreed that the 'shape' (within which Anglicans would want to set the ordained ministry) of the Church is not arbitrary.[22]

Long ago, Friedrich Schleiermacher distinguished between Catholic and Protestant sensibilities to the Church: the former made the Christian dependent on Christ through the Church; the latter made the Christian dependent on the Church through Christ.[23] Is this still where we remain? Is there not truth in both? Can there be an authentic ecclesial mediation of faith? Without *some* sense of the ecclesial mediation of faith we are surely locked into an individualism that ultimately destroys any sense of Church. The ecclesiological study, which is surely called for, must have as broad an ecumenical base as possible if it is to make headway with this question. Volf's study offers us a model. It is, in effect, a tripartite dialogue between Catholic, Orthodox and Protestant voices. With his 'partners' in dialogue (Ratzinger and Zizioulas), Volf believes individualism to be destructive not only of the Church, but also ultimately of the 'givenness' of revelation. Volf's own constructive work on the ecclesial mediation of faith would be no bad starting point. He believes Schleiermacher's distinction to be perceptive but simplistic. Faith is the work of God's Spirit. It is to be received not in pure passivity but with receptive activity. Addressing the question of the instrumentality (and thus sacramentality) of the Church, Volf rejects the direct, that is the totally unmediated, action of God upon the soul. So:

> God's salvific activity always takes place through the multidirectional confession of faith of the *communio fidelium*. The sacraments, which no person can self-administer and yet which each person must receive personally, symbolize most clearly the essential communal character of the mediation of faith.[24]

There is also an opening of discussion on the instrumentality of the Church in *The Church of Jesus Christ*.[25] What, according to Volf, the Church does not mediate is the Spirit's internal gift of personal trust, *fiducia*. Volf also carefully expounds a Protestant understanding of Christ *alone* as the subject of all salvific activity, though he notes that there is an ecumenical consensus with the Roman Catholic Church that Christ is the *real* subject of salvation. The remaining (and important question) is not so much whether the Church is instrumental in Christ's salvation, but the character of such instrumentality.[26] Part of the argument here, and the part most relevant for our ecumenical impasse, is whether or not offices in the Church – ministry, episcopacy, councils, Papacy – guarantee the transmission of the truth of the gospel over and above the wider *sensus fidelium*. For Volf the answer must clearly be 'No'; as it is clearly 'Yes' in the ecclesiology of Cardinal Ratzinger. Is *fiducia* something that can be given through external offices of the Church, or only, as Volf argues, personally to the Christian as a member of Christ's faithful? However strongly most Anglicans would wish to insist on a certain, real, ecclesial instrumentality, and thus the sacramentality of the Church (whether or not that term is used), our recent official formulations have explicitly repudiated the idea that office *guarantees* fidelity. As the House of Bishops' Statement *Apostolicity and Succession* puts it (quoting the Porvoo Common Statement): 'The use of the sign of the historic episcopal succession does not by itself guarantee the fidelity of a church to every aspect of apostolic faith, life and mission.'[27]

Significantly for wider future ecumenical consensus, Cardinal Walter Kasper has similarly stated that offices are 'no guarantee for the actual transmission of the gospel'.[28] If office in the Church is understood to guarantee something in a mechanistic or automatic sense irrespective of faith serious problems arise.

an episodic Church?

In an ecumenical study of the ecclesial mediation of faith there is a further matter that will need attention. This will be requested by Christian traditions that have stressed the 'closeness' of Christ to the Church rather than those which wish to maintain a 'distance'. Anglicans will be among such who would welcome an ecumenical consensus on how ecclesial 'actualism' is to be avoided, in those ecclesiologies that emphasize (correctly enough) the reality of failure and sin within the Church. This would be an ecclesiology where the Church apparently exists only at certain 'moments', an episodic Church. Such a view has popular 'Protestant' expression in the belief that the Church disappeared from view during many centuries of decay and corruption only to 'reappear' with Martin Luther or the Pentecostal movement. It can also have other more surprising expressions: John Zizioulas' eucharistic theology of the local church can be read as suggesting that between eucharistic assemblies the people are not Church, though I am sure he does not intend such a reading.[29] The more the *absolute* necessity for an ordained ministry is stressed for the performance of the sacraments, the more even a Catholic ecclesiology faces the risk of a practical 'liminalism' among communities suffering a prolonged absence of priests.

But to invest the ontological continuity of the Church in the episcopate risks what our partners fear: not only a kind of 'condensing' of the Spirit into a structure but also a radical and un-scriptural division among the baptized between those in whom ecclesial continuity is 'embodied' and the remainder who become the 'non-essential' Church. Perhaps an ecumenical exploration of a *baptismal* ecclesiology of communion coupled with the theology of justification would lead to positive results. The grounding of the continuing identity of the Church must be in Christ's presence among all his people by the power of the Spirit. Baptism as well as the Eucharist is the sign of this because, amongst other things, it manifests the permanent status of the Christian as an adopted child of God in the community of the forgiveness of sins and is thus a proclamation of our right standing before God. For Augustine baptism was the Sacrament of Justification, and the homily *Of the Salvation of Mankind* also makes this Augustinian emphasis.[30] Ecumenical discussion of the New Testament meaning of justification and baptism into the Body of Christ could offer fresh insight into the question of the continuing visibility of the Church. Be that as it may, it is at this point in the argument and not before that the office of the ministry is seen; in service of Word and

Sacrament which constitute the Church. In spite of the need to avoid 'actualism', no ministry can be construed as in itself constitutive of the Church.

ecclesiologies as ecclesiastical apologia?

A final prolegomenal marker concerns our motives in the choice of one ecclesiology rather than another, granted the plurality of metaphors for the Church in the New Testament. Do we in fact subconsciously choose an ecclesiology because of an intuition that it will buttress our existing church practice? Ecclesiologies invariably seem to portray a Church remarkably like the confessional allegiance of their authors: even Volf's genuinely ecumenical ecclesiology endorses his Congregationalism, albeit with significant 'Catholic' and 'Orthodox' modifications! Anglican ecclesiologies have certainly inhabited Anglican glass houses!

A related comment can be made about the diverse ecclesiologies that refer to the *koinonia* of the Holy Trinity. In his thorough examination of Ratzinger's and Zizioulas' ecclesiologies, Volf argues that their differing approaches, Western and Eastern, are respective reflections of the Western and Eastern doctrines of the Holy Trinity. He himself expresses a third understanding of the *koinonia* of the Trinity that his own ecclesiology of the *local* church then similarly echoes. The question arises: do we shape our ecclesiology or even our Trinitarian theology according to our ecclesial praxis?

showing catholicity

In sketching both a conclusion (to this book) and an ecumenical prognosis, I have taken a somewhat circuitous route to the question: do bishops obscure the unity of the Church or do they (rightly understood) exhibit it; do they hold out the unity of the Church so as to be seen? I have been exploring some of the reasons why our Evangelical ecumenical partners do not find our oft repeated insistence on the full, visible unity of the Church as straightforward a dogmatic proposition as most Anglicans have found heretofore, still less that it entails episcopacy.

When the first Tractarians defended the Church of England against intrusion by what was already 'secular' government, they knew that many people thought of the established Church not as a spiritual society, not as that part of the one, holy, catholic and apostolic

Church of Jesus Christ which is in England, but rather as an ecclesiastical arm of the state. To lay claim to be the Church of the Apostles rather than a sub-department of the Home Office, the Tractarians spoke of 'our apostolical descent'.[31] Since then Anglican apologia for episcopacy has frequently concentrated on such descent. But the *reductio ad absurdum* of such argument can be seen in the *episcopi vagantes* sects. Unbroken episcopal lineage does not necessarily mean an authentic *ecclesia*. Michael Ramsey's *The Gospel and the Catholic Church* was published in 1936. In a sustained argument he made an elegant plea for relating episcopacy to the gospel rather than pedigree: though he was second to none in his insistence that the Church is a historical community in continuity with the Word made flesh.[32] He was not arguing for episcopacy *alone* but an 'evangelical' order of Scripture, sacraments, episcopacy and creeds. He articulated his anxieties about the popular Anglican understanding of 'apostolic succession' by carefully expounding an Irenaean doctrine of Scripture and the succession of apostolic Churches represented through their bishops. Representative bishops *with* Bibles *teaching* their Churches this doctrine! Ramsey also distanced himself from the prevailing Anglo-Catholic view of the necessity of episcopal ordination for 'validating' ministry, by recognizing the 'experience' and 'power' of the ministry of the Protestant Churches.[33] In commending episcopacy on evangelical grounds he invited Anglicans to avoid merely historical argument.[34] Ramsey's invitation to engage in an evangelical argument for episcopacy was not substantially taken up. Indeed, in 1947 *The Apostolic Ministry*[35] was published and that collection of essays will probably remain both the best and the last of an almost purely historical argument for episcopacy as necessary for church order.

In looking to the future with our ecumenical partners in Churches that do not 'possess' episcopacy we would do well to set on one side questions of history until some of the more fundamental ecclesiological questions have been resolved. With Ramsey and the Apostolic Fathers we would do better to explore together the meaning of the *catholicity* of the Church. Catholicity and episcopacy indeed come together early enough for the first use of the word *catholic* is found in Ignatius' letter to the Smyrnians commending episcopacy.[36] Though there is a continuous history of interpretation of the meaning of catholicity in this context, we could well start from the undisputed dictum of Karl Barth that the Church is 'catholic, or it is not the Church'.[37] John Webster suggests we look again at Karl Barth on the visibility of the Church and explore more deeply how forms of unity, including ministry and *episcope*, can *show* the invisible rather than apparently replace the invisible.[38]

local church and universal Church

A number of issues would need to be attended to within a study of catholicity as part of a wider ecumenical project on ecclesiology and the visibility of the Church. Not least the *location* of the Church. There appears to be a significant consensus about the ecclesiological significance of the local church. Orthodox, Roman Catholics, Anglicans and Protestants would generally wish to avoid the implication that the universal Church is represented locally merely by local sub-units.[39] This, curiously, appears to have been Michael Ramsey's view for he spoke of the episcopate as representing the universal Church and of the local church only as part of the primary universal Church.[40] Yet the logical consequences of such a view, in the end, can only be ultramontane: a universal bishop for the single universal Church. If there is, conversely, a real ecumenical consensus that the fullness of the Church of Christ is truly present in each local church the problem facing ecclesiology is the other way round. Should we not all be Congregationalists? The problem for the Congregational Church is how it can express its catholicity: otherwise there is no unity beyond the congregation at all and we are left with ecclesiologically independent units: 'Is Christ divided?' could only be asked within a single congregation. A communion ecclesiology therefore requires a linkage between local churches (however 'local' is defined: congregation, diocese or regional church) and other Churches. This link can be collegial, as in the presbytery or consistory of the Reformed tradition; or personal and collegial in episcopal Churches. It can also be conciliar and synodal as in almost all Churches with forms of national or wider structure such as a General Assembly or General Synod. There can also be personal expressions of unity at national or international levels: as in all episcopal primacies, including the Papacy, but also in weaker forms such as moderators or chairpersons of councils. All are ways of expressing communion and interrelationships: the connexion in the Methodist sense. All are ways of making and exhibiting a wider catholicity between the Churches and thus witnessing to the *oneness* of Christ's Church in its local plurality. Episcopacy must be seen alongside other providentially given instruments of unity such as collegiality, conciliarity or synodality: to all of which episcopacy relates historically and dogmatically.

linking the local and wider Churches

Before taking the discussion about episcopacy further, an ecumenical consensus would need to be established that whatever level of unity Christians speak of, local or wider, its inner, invisible bonding is the Spirit of Christ. Just as the reality of the local church is constituted by the presence of Christ through the Spirit in Word and Sacrament, so the same invisible Spirit is constitutive of all wider communion between local churches. As the local church is seen in Word and Sacrament, an outward and visible sign of an invisible reality, so the *communion* of the local churches, itself an invisible reality, is shown in forms of *episcope*, corporate and personal and most fully focused in the episcopate. But just as the ordained ministry is not constitutive of the Church as such at the local level, neither at the wider level of communion between local churches is the episcopate constitutive of this communion, which is always of the Spirit. It does, however, exhibit the network of communion in time and space we call catholicity, the 'visibility', the 'holding forth to be seen' of the essential relationship between one local church and another.

I have been suggesting earlier that we must listen with some theological attentiveness to what our ecumenical partners are saying about the sufficiency of unity in an assembly of Christians where the Word is proclaimed and the sacraments celebrated: Augsburg's *satis est*. We can understand the contention that the *quality* of such local unity and communion with God and our fellow Christians cannot be improved, nor its visibility further enhanced at the congregational level. Nevertheless, to be truly the Church of Christ a local church must seek a wider connectedness. What kind of status does this connectedness have; what kind of communion is communion *between* churches; is *intra*communion within a (local) church to be distinguished from *inter*communion between local churches? Is there a distinction to be drawn between different registers of communion analogous to a distinction that can also be drawn between degrees of ecclesiality? Is there not here a different register of ecclesial communion? (It must always be emphasized that unity and communion at either the local or wider levels is present as an eschatological rather than complete reality.) André Birmelé has expressed something like this in a comparison between the Meissen and Porvoo agreements:

> There is indubitably a scale of visibility. With regard to the visibility of unity the Porvoo Agreement represents a clear advance on Meissen. The jointly exercised *episcope* leads

to a more visible unity than is the case in Meissen or even in Leuenberg. For this reason – particularly in the latter two cases – additional signs of visibility must still be achieved.[41]

Anglicans have said that a Church is most truly itself when it celebrates the Eucharist and that when a bishop visits a parish, preaches and presides as chief minister of Word and Sacrament such a Church is fully itself.[42] Such a community does not cease to be the Church at other times, nor does it cease to be catholic, but its catholicity is then exhibited in an indirect way through the delegated ministry of the presbyter. But whether bishop or presbyter presides over Word and Sacrament they are a visible sign of the catholicity of the Church, which is itself constituted by the Spirit through Word and Sacrament.

what kind of sign?

If there is a case for such differentiation, it may be helpful in framing future Anglican discourse about episcopacy. Contemporary Anglican explanation of episcopacy in part has already shifted from arguments based on historic succession to the signification of catholicity. Bishops are said to be 'signs' of both diachronic and synchronic catholicity.[43] The difficulty about such language for our partners, at least in part, may well be in the whole cluster of meanings which 'sign' represents in such a complex context. When a bishop presides over the Eucharist, *the sign* of Christ's catholic presence, it is not the bishop as an individual but the whole assembly of the Church celebrating Word and Sacrament which is *the sacrament of unity*. The bishop is not a personal sacrament, not *the* sign in the sense that he constitutes the Church. He (or she) does however, as do all ordained ministers, *serve* the constitutive work of Word and Sacrament in a distinct and special way, even instrumentally, as Calvin himself indicated.[44]

It is not in dispute ecumenically that the office of the ministry is a 'bond by which believers are kept together in one Body'.[45] Thus all ordained ministry normally has a service of wider unity and catholicity. This is especially so for all supra-congregational ministry. The ministry of oversight (*episcope*) takes many forms. Titles such as superintendent, *inspecteur ecclesiastique*, *Oberkirchenrat*, moderator and even district chairperson have an ecclesial significance. It is in the context of synchronic catholicity that such personal ministries, especially the episcopate, can legitimately be said to be a theological and practical sign of unity, though at another level or register from Word and Sacrament.

sign of the future

Diachronic catholicity not only reintroduces the question of history but must also introduce eschatology. The Anglican preoccupation with the episcopate in history has become unbalanced precisely because it has not considered the catholicity of the future as well as that of the past: Christ is the Omega as well as the Alpha.[46] What does it mean to think of episcopacy as a sign of the *future* catholicity God intends for his Church and all creation? Nevertheless, as Anglicans reconsider a commendation of episcopacy in terms of diachronic catholicity we shall have to give more thought to the ambiguities of past history. Geoffrey Wainwright has asked with characteristic clarity what the theological practical significance of unfaithful bishops is in matters of episcopal succession.[47] What is the sign value when history has shown bishops to be not just obscuring unity but to be obstacles to the gospel? Perhaps we need an ecumenical discussion of the wider theological principle asserted in Article XXVI of the Anglican Articles of Religion that the unworthiness of the minister does not hinder the effect of the sacrament: that is to say an exploration of how the Body of Christ still witnesses to its Head in spite of human sin among its ministers and members. A related problem with the history of episcopacy is that for over four hundred years some Churches have been without it. How can episcopacy have diachronic sign value for such Churches? Yet such Churches have not been without a ministry of oversight (*episcope*), as Anglicans have long recognized.[48] Such ministries of oversight, albeit not in the distinct episcopal order, Anglicans believe to be part of God's will for the Church. Could such existing ministries of wider oversight, whether personal or corporate, be set in a similar frame of reference to that within which Anglicans would wish to place the episcopate, that is, as exhibiting catholic unity? Moreover, there would be great value at this point in exploring the *ecclesial intentionality* of such ministers of oversight. Bearing in mind that diachronic catholicity includes an eschatological reference to the future as well as to the past, what Churches solemnly *intend* by prayer (as in an ordination rite) is a datum of what they actually *are* eschatologically through the Spirit. In Catholic theology there is an analogy to this in the doctrine of desire. A person sincerely wishes to be baptized but is prevented: that person is said to receive all the grace of baptism 'by desire'. In the case of ministries of oversight in the 'non-episcopal' Churches there is indeed actual ordination and it typically includes the idea of catholic unity and its service.

catholicity as an obligation to openness

Such a framework of synchronic and diachronic catholicity as the reference for both episcopal and other ministries intending *episcope* – including corporate forms of *episcope* – presupposes a more general intention towards catholicity. How is this to be determined? Volf's discussion of the marks of catholicity is instructive. From his perspective he understandably rejects the necessity for juridical communion with Rome as the guarantee of catholicity. Nor the absolute indispensability of formal communion with other local Churches in space and time through the historic episcopate, desirable as such may be. He proposes that the minimum requirement of catholicity should be an *openness* to other Churches. Churches that close themselves off from other Churches deny their catholicity:

> A church cannot reflect the eschatological catholicity of the entire people of God and at the same time isolate itself from other churches. *The catholicity of the local church presupposes that the channels for synchronic and diachronic communication between all churches remain open.*[49] (emphasis mine)

If this at first sounds a little too easy, a little like the 'reconciled diversity' that even some Lutherans are becoming suspicious of,[50] or a complacent interpretation of Augsburg's *satis est*, Volf continues with an emphatic insistence that we are not entitled to rest with minimum catholicity. I have, in any case, been suggesting in addition that any ecclesial ministries that point to wider oversight are indicative of an intentional catholicity. But Volf continues by solemnly urging the *optimum* rather than minimum expression of catholicity:

> *Every catholic church is charged with maintaining and deepening its ties to other churches past and present.* The church that refuses to do thus would not be a church at all. Openness to other churches should lead to a free networking with those churches, and as the image of the net also suggests, *these mutual relations should be expressed in corresponding ecclesial institutions.*[51] (emphasis mine)

He concludes by speaking of loyalty to the Apostolic Tradition as the basic identifying feature of catholicity: that is to say, the 'historically mediated apostolic scripture'.

Volf's return to the linkage between catholicity and apostolicity is both Irenaean (and the emphasis of Michael Ramsey) and ecumenically constructive at this point of my somewhat dispersed argument. Anglican historicism in relation to the apostolicity of the Church has not been helpful or authentically historical: the argument in effect has been that a Church is catholic and therefore authentic because it is apostolic, that is episcopal. But it is rather the other way round: a Church is apostolic and therefore authentic because it is open to other Churches which are also endeavouring in the Spirit to receive from the past, interpret today and hand on for the future the Apostolic Tradition. This openness to other Churches requires a network of communion between Churches. This has been embodied in a number of forms; the exchange of apostolic letters, the reception of the canon, the sharing of the liturgical reading of Scripture, the influence of liturgy, spirituality and the saints; and especially the *episcope* of the ordained ministry in its ever changing forms. But within the latter a collegiality and conciliar episcopacy (as opposed to an isolated *episcopus* whether in a single-bishop sect or an ultramontane Papacy) can be argued to be the most appropriate way of sharing the network of the catholicity of the Church. It is not the only way, nor a guaranteed way of achieving catholicity and thus discerning apostolicity. It is a way, however, that Anglicans – and Orthodox and Roman Catholics – may wish to present to our Evangelical partners if they wish to examine the question against the widest possible horizon: global Christianity *and* two millennia of Christian success and failure. It will, however, require horizons beyond that of any one confession, national Church, or even world denomination.

In a prescient essay, Rowan Williams warns of the temptation to Christians of retreating into an inner life of prayer, sacrament and sanctification and dismissing the organizational side of the Church:

> The retreat into the Small Group is a simple solution, but one which runs against all that the idea of 'catholicity' has positively meant for the Church: the mutual critical openness of the local body and the wider structure, the reciprocal nourishment offered by particular local communities. And if catholicity matters, structures of authority matter.[52]

Significantly, quoting Zizioulas, Williams continues by arguing that it is precisely because of the bishop's ministry as chief minister of Word and Sacrament, demonstrated in his eucharistic presidency (or in his delegation or sharing of that role), that the bishop's function is to 'make the catholicity of the Church reveal itself in a certain place'.[53] It is to be noted that the Zizioulas quotation by Williams does not suggest the bishop *is* the catholicity, but rather that catholicity reveals 'itself' through the ministry of the bishop in service of Word and Sacrament. Williams concludes this part of his argument as follows:

> And the bishop is equipped to do this because he is 'put there' by the Church to focus its unity in presiding at the common meal. At this level, he is (as we have noted) himself a symbol. He does not have power over the community, far less power over the symbol; [*Here, Williams means the proclamation of the Scriptures and the celebration of the sacraments through which Christ encounters his people*] rather he becomes part of the symbolic mediation by which the Church renews its encounter with what creates it and sustains it – the grace of Christ. And anything that needs to be said about succession, legitimation, continuity of tradition, and so forth must be spelled out in relation to this symbolic sense of ministerial order: if a bishop is truly to unveil the catholicity of the local church, he cannot depend for his ordination only on the local and the contemporary, he must visibly belong in a community extended in time and space beyond the local.[54]

conclusion

An ecumenical study of catholicity, within a wider study of ecclesiology and visibility taking into account the insights and convictions of the Catholic, Orthodox and Protestant ecclesiological traditions, could be the appropriate context to look again at episcopacy as exhibiting, showing, though not guaranteeing catholicity. One consequence of this might be the recognition that there *are* different, though not necessarily incompatible, understandings of visibility. Those who adhere to the Reformation ecclesiological grammar would normally understand the visibility of the Church with reference to that which constitutes the Church: Word and Sacrament. Anglicans would wish to understand the meaning of full, visible unity both locally and wider within the register of the full catholicity of the Church – because no local Church can be truly itself without openness and interconnectedness with others – and hence wish to commend the episcopate as well as other forms of oversight as part of what catholic unity entails. Some mutual understandings would necessarily be required, not least that a wrong understanding of the ecclesial mediation of salvation had been ruled out. Episcopacy would also need to be commended in a very carefully framed context so as to avoid the implication that it is needed for the validation of past or present ministry, or that it is being used as a trans-temporal bridge to the days of the 'undivided' Church in such a way as to ignore or bypass the experience of grace in the interim. But rather, it would be seen in the spirit of openness to other Churches that Volf characterizes as catholicity. Episcopacy in such a context would be seen and welcomed by a Church as part of its *essential* evangelical and catholic task of 'maintaining and deepening its ties to other churches past and present' – a renewed and ecumenical episcopacy as part of a network of catholicity to exhibit the communion of the *una sancta*.

Notes

Foreword

1 Paul Avis in 'Rethinking Ecumenical Theology', p. 96.
2 *Towards a Church of England Response to BEM and ARCIC* (GS 661), Church Information Office, 1985, pp. 6, 7.

Chapter 1

1 For background, see M. Tanner, 'The Goal of Unity in Theological Dialogues involving Anglicans', in G. Gassmann and P. Nørgaard-Højen (eds), *Einheit der Kirche*, O. Lembeck, 1988, pp. 69–78; M. Tanner, 'The Ecumenical Future', in S.W. Sykes and John Booty (eds), *The Study of Anglicanism*, SPCK, 1998, pp. 427–46; M. Root, '"Reconciled diversity" and the visible church', in C. Podmore (ed.), *Community – Unity – Communion: Essays in Honour of Mary Tanner*, Church House Publishing, 1998, pp. 237–51.
2 A. C. Clark and C. Davey (eds), *Anglican/Roman Catholic Dialogue: The Work of the Preparatory Commission*, Oxford University Press, 1974, p. 2.
3 The New Delhi Report, paragraph 116, *New Delhi Speaks*, SCM Press, 1962, p. 55.
4 The Nairobi Report, D. M. Paton (ed.), *Breaking Barriers: Nairobi 1975*, SPCK/Eerdmans, 1976, p. 60.
5 Anglican–Roman Catholic International Commission (ARCIC), *The Final Report*, CTS/SPCK, 1982, Introduction, paragraph 9.
6 Second Anglican–Roman Catholic International Commission, *Salvation and the Church*, ACC/Secretariat for Promoting Christian Unity, 1987, Preface, p. 7.
7 *The Niagara Report: Report of the Anglican–Lutheran Consultation on Episcope 1987*, Church House Publishing, 1988, paragraph 71.
8 *The Meissen Agreement*, London: Council for Christian Unity, 1992, paragraphs 7f.; cf. Reuilly Common Statement: *Called to Witness and Service*, Church House Publishing, 1999, paragraphs 21–5; Fetter Lane Common Statement, *Anglican–Moravian Conversations*, London, Council for Christian Unity of the General Synod, 1996, paragraphs 24–7.

9   *God's Reign and Our Unity*, SPCK/St Andrew Press, 1984, paragraph 29.
10 ARCIC II, *Salvation and the Church*, p. 7.
11 *The Niagara Report*, paragraph 15; cf. paragraph 35.
12 Meissen Agreement, paragraphs 3, 7; cf. Reuilly Common Statement, paragraphs 16–18.
13 ARCIC I, *The Final Report*, Introduction, paragraph 5.
14 *Towards a CofE Response to BEM and ARCIC*, Church House Publishing, 1985, paragraph 1.
15 ARCIC II, *Salvation and the Church*, paragraph 1.
16 Meissen Agreement, paragraph 4.
17 M. Root, 'The Unity of the Church and the Reality of the Denominations', *Modern Theology* 9, 1993, pp. 385–401.
18 A. Birmelé, 'The Unity of the Church', in Podmore (ed.), *Community – Unity – Communion*, p. 260.
19 I. U. Dalferth, 'Ministry and the Office of the Bishop according to Meissen and Porvoo: Protestant Remarks about Several Unclarified Questions', in *Visible Unity and the Ministry of Oversight. The Second Theological Conference held under the Meissen Agreement between the Church of England and the Evangelical Church in Germany*, Church House Publishing, 1997, pp. 9–48.
20 K. Barth, *Church Dogmatics* IV/1, T&T Clark, 1956, p. 654.
21 Barth, *Church Dogmatics* IV/1, p. 658.
22 A bad example is the rather muddled treatment of 'The Church as Creation of the Word and of the Holy Spirit' in the WCC paper *The Nature and Purpose of the Church*, WCC Publications, 1998, which (in paragraphs 9–12) gives a clear account of the fact that, generated by Word and Spirit, the Church 'cannot exist by and for itself' (paragraph 9) but then shifts without further ado to emphasize that the Church is its members 'common partaking in God's own life whose innermost being is communion. Thus it is a divine and human reality' (paragraph 13), and proceeds to give a substantial exposition of *koinonia* ecclesiology (paragraphs 48ff.).
23 Worries on this score lie behind the rejection of the *Joint Declaration* by Lutheran theologians unconvinced by their fellow Lutherans' reading of the New Testament and Luther: see E. Jüngel, *Justification: The Heart of the Christian Faith*, T&T Clark, 2001.
24 Meissen Agreement, paragraph 7.
25 Finely emphasized by Brian Beck, '"Until we all attain": Eschatology and the goal of unity', in Podmore (ed.), *Community – Unity – Communion*, pp. 227–36.

26 G. Evans, *Method in Ecumenical Theology*, Cambridge University Press, 1996, p. 223.

Chapter 2

1 Many dialogues have issued in 'Common Statements' (e.g. ARCIC, Fetter Lane, Porvoo, Reuilly) or 'Agreements' (Meissen), some in 'Reports' (e.g. *God's Reign and Our Unity, Anglican–Lutheran Dialogue*). These common titles disguise substantial differences in style and content (e.g. as between the slightly magisterial style and relatively detailed *content* of ARCIC and the more conversational and generalized character of Fetter Lane or Reuilly).

2 Meaning that the initial formal Conversations are complete, though there may be a continuing process of 'follow-up' between the Churches concerned.

3 For example, some traditions or Churches see it as proper to acknowledge past error in ways which others believe to be inappropriate. The difference will have an obvious bearing on ecumenical agreement.

4 *An Anglican–Methodist Covenant*, Methodist Publishing House/Church House Publishing, 2001. The Covenant document also includes a sensitive statement on 'The Healing of Memories' (see pp. 2f., 14f.).

5 See, e.g., Fetter Lane Common Statement, *Anglican–Moravian Conversations*, London, Council for Christian Unity of the General Synod, 1996, Chapter VI.

6 The Helsinki Statement, *Anglican–Lutheran Dialogue: The Report of the Anglican–Lutheran European Regional Commission*, SPCK, 1983, p. 29.

7 John Paul II, 1980, cf. The Malta Report, 1967, paragraphs 3 & 4 in A. C. Clark and C. Davey (eds), *Anglican/Roman Catholic Dialogue: The Work of the Preparatory Commission*, Oxford University Press, 1974, p. 108. In one sense it is natural for Churches which can trace their separation from a specific past era (such as the Reformation of the sixteenth century) to seek a 'way back' to truths once held in common. However, the methodology of ARCIC has not – for good reasons – focused on pre-Reformation doctrine but on the attempt to find some more pristine and fundamental basis for shared doctrine: see, e.g., the treatment of the presence of Christ and the doctrine of transubstantiation in the statement on the Eucharist.

8 See, for example, the section on 'Koinonia and Mission' in

An Anglican–Methodist Covenant, p. 28 (and p. 29), and the exposition of 'Communion' in the ARCIC II Agreed Statement: Second Anglican–Roman Catholic International Commission, *Church as Communion*, Church House Publishing/CTS, 1991.

9   ARCIC II, *Life in Christ: Morals, Communion and the Church*, ACC/Pontifical Council for Promoting Christian Unity, 1994, p. 30.

10   *God's Reign and Our Unity*, SPCK/St Andrew Press, 1984, p. 64.

11   ARCIC II, *The Gift of Authority: Authority in the Church III*, CTS/Church House Publishing, 1999, p. 24.

12   *Towards Visible Unity*, 1980, p. 64.

13   *The Gift of Authority,* pp. 15 [paragraphs 12 & 13] and 35–6 [paragraph 49]; cf. also the role ascribed to the *sensus fidei* of every Christian as contributing to the formation of the *sensus fidelium* of the Church as a whole.

14   '. . . the unicity of the Church founded by [Christ] must be *firmly believed* as a truth of Catholic faith. Just as there is one Christ, so there exists a single body of Christ, a single Bride of Christ; "A single Catholic and Apostolic Church".' The Declaration of the Vatican Congregation for the Doctrine of the Faith, *Dominus Jesus* section IV, Offices of the Congregation for the Doctrine of the Faith, Rome, 2000.

15   *Anglican–Orthodox Dialogue: The Moscow Agreed Statement*, SPCK, 1977, pp. 84–5.

16   *Anglican–Orthodox Dialogue: The Dublin Agreed Statement 1984*, SPCK, 1985, p. 29.

17   Dublin Agreed Statement, p. 45.

18   Anglican–Roman Catholic International Commission (ARCIC), *The Final Report*, CTS/SPCK, 1982, p. 110.

19   ARCIC I, *The Final Report*, paragraph 6.

20   ARCIC I, *The Final Report*, p. 16.

21   ARCIC I, *The Final Report*, p. 24.

22   'What we have to say represents the consensus of the Commission on essential matters where it considers that doctrine admits no divergence': ARCIC I, *The Final Report*, p. 38.

23   ARCIC I, *The Final Report*, p. 63.

24   *Church as Communion*, p. 35.

25   *Life in Christ*, p. 12.

26   *Life in Christ*, p. 18.

27   *Life in Christ*, p. 30.

28   *The Gift of Authority*, pp. 22–3.

29   Though the paragraph cited finds a brief echo in the section on Primacy: 'This sort of primacy will already assist the Church on earth to be the authentic catholic *koinonia* in which unity does

not curtail diversity, and diversity does not endanger but enhances unity.' *The Gift of Authority*, p. 42 [paragraph 60].

30 Though the style of *Life in Christ* is marked by a more tentative and narrative flavour.

31 E.g. 'Within both churches different attitudes exist concerning the nature of inspiration.' *Anglican–Lutheran International Conversations 1970–1972*, SPCK, 1973, p. 9.

32 'What difference of theological emphasis remains we regard as not serious enough to divide our Churches.' *The Helsinki Statement*, p. 29.

33 'Like any living being, the Church only remains what it is through change and adjustment.' *The Niagara Report: Report of the Anglican–Lutheran Consultation on Episcope 1987*, Church House Publishing, 1988, p. 19.

34 The Meissen Agreement, Council for Christian Unity, 1992, p. 10. The theme of cultural diversity is taken up again in the later section (p. 16) on Agreement in Faith: 'We also rejoice at the variety of expression shown in different cultural settings.'

35 The Porvoo Common Statement, *Commitment to Mission and Unity*, Church House Publishing, 1993, pp. 13–14.

36 *Towards Visible Unity*, p. 64.

37 *Towards Visible Unity*, p. 64.

38 *God's Reign and Our Unity*, p. 16.

39 *God's Reign and Our Unity*, pp. 66–7.

40 Fetter Lane Common Statement, p. 28.

41 Fetter Lane Common Statement, p. 29.

42 *Facing Unity: Models, Forms and Phases of Catholic–Lutheran Church Fellowship*, Report of the Roman Catholic–Lutheran Joint Commission, Lutheran World Federation, 1985.

43 Reuilly Common Statement: *Called to Witness and Service*, Church House Publishing and Methodist Publishing House, 1996, p. 22. NB The comparable paragraph in the Report of the Informal Conversations between the Methodist Church and the Church of England, *Commitment to Mission and Unity*, Church House Publishing/Methodist Publishing House, 1996, represents a similar catena.

44 Reuilly Common Statement, p. 23.

45 E.g. with relation to the Diaconate, non-presbyteral presidency at the Eucharist and the place of women in Episcopal ministry (*An Anglican–Methodist Covenant*, pp. 46 and 49).

46 *An Anglican–Methodist Covenant*, p. 33.

47 Except indirectly, by reference to the place of 'reception' in the life of the Church, as in *The Gift of Authority*.

48 Although *The Gift of Authority* has a brief paragraph on

'Discipline: The Exercise on Authority and the Freedom of Conscience', in which it is asserted that 'The exercise of authority must always respect conscience, because the divine work of salvation affirms human freedom' (p. 35, paragraph 49), there is little development of this theme and its implications.

49   John Zizioulas, *Being as Communion: Studies in Personhood and the Church*, Darton, Longman & Todd, 1985.

50   A trend further encouraged (in these islands, at least) by the British Council of Churches' Study Commission Report, *The Forgotten Trinity*, British Council of Churches, 1989.

51   Among recent critical reflections on this tendency in theology, see Harriet Harris, 'Should we say that Personhood is Relational?', *Scottish Journal of Theology* 51, 1998; Karen Kilby, 'Perichoresis and Projection: Problems with the Social Doctrine of the Trinity', *New Blackfriars*, October 2000; Nicholas Sagovsky, *Ecumenism, Christian Origins and the Practice of Communion*, Cambridge University Press, 2000; and Peter Fisher, 'Koinonia and Conflict', *Theology* CIV No. 822, November 2001.

52   Or at least only in the most paradoxical sense, as when Moltmann, drawing on Luther and others, writes of the 'trial between God and God' which takes place at the crucifixion. Jürgen Moltmann, *The Crucified God*, SCM Press, 1974, pp. 152f.

53   Nicholas M. Healy, *Church, World and the Christian Life: Practical-Prophetic Ecclesiology,* Cambridge University Press, 2000, p. 37. See also pp. 44ff. for his comments on 'Communion' ecclesiologies.

54   'One of the urgent needs of the church these days is to understand the ecclesial significance of controversy. To put it more plainly, we need to remember that conflict in the church is not necessarily a matter of revolt against and defence of a settled solution, but a God-given means of discovering what we actually believe.' Rowan Williams in a review article in *Scottish Journal of Theology* 56, 2003, p. 92.

Chapter 3

1   *The Church of England Year Book 2001*, Church House Publishing, 2001, p. 405.

2   G. K. A. Bell, *Christian Unity – The Anglican Position*, Hodder & Stoughton, 1948.

3   R. Coleman (ed.), *Resolutions of the Twelve Lambeth Conferences 1867–1988*, Anglican Book Centre, 1992, p. 13.

4   Coleman (ed.), *Resolutions*, pp. 46–7.

5   Reuilly Common Statement: *Called to Witness and Service*, Church House Publishing, 1999, p. 23.

6   E. J. Bicknell, *The Thirty-Nine Articles of the Church of England*, ed. H. J. Carpenter, 3rd rev. edn, Longmans, Green, 1955, p. 244.

7   Bicknell, *The Thirty-Nine Articles*, p. 244.

8   A. M. Ramsey, *The Gospel and the Catholic Church*, Longmans, Green, 1936, p. 50.

9   A. C. Headlam, *The Doctrine of the Church and Reunion*, John Murray, 1923, p. 281.

10 J. Macquarrie, *Principles of Christian Theology*, 2nd edn, SCM Press, 1977, pp. 41–2.

11 W. H. Griffith Thomas, *The Principles of Theology*, Church Book Room Press, 1951, p. 276.

12 A. M. Stibbs, 'The Unity of All In Each Place', in J. I. Packer (ed.), *All in Each Place*, The Marcham Manor Press, 1965, pp. 57–8.

13 J. I. Packer, 'The Doctrine and Expression of Christian Unity', in J. I. Packer, *Serving the People of God*, Paternoster Press, 1998, p. 39.

14 Packer, 'The Doctrine and Expression of Christian Unity', p. 42. It is interesting to note that the classic Reformation basis for unity advocated by Packer is that followed by the continental Lutheran and Reformed Churches who have signed up to the Leuenberg agreement, and that Packer's criticism of the Anglican ecumenical approach has been echoed by the Church of England's ecumenical partners in the EKD and in the French Lutheran and Reformed Churches.

15 E. L. Mascall, *Corpus Christi*, Longmans, Green, 1953, p. 13.

16 Mascall, *Corpus Christi*, p. 19.

17 Headlam, *The Doctrine of the Church*, p. 268.

18 G. T. Manley, *Christian Unity*, IVF, 1945, pp. 36–7.

19 M. Green, *Freed to Serve*, Hodder & Stoughton, 1983, p. 71.

20 M. Tinker, 'Towards an Evangelical View of the Church', in M. Tinker (ed.), *The Anglican Evangelical Crisis*, Christian Focus Publications, 1996, p. 106.

21 Tinker, 'Towards an Evangelical View of the Church', p. 106.

22 NEAC1, Keele 1967, 'The Church and its Unity', paragraph 88.

23 D. Watson, *I Believe in the Church*, Hodder & Stoughton, 1978, p. 343

24 Watson, *I Believe in the Church*, p. 353.

25 G. Carey, *The Meeting of the Waters*, Hodder & Stoughton, 1985, pp. 158–9.
26 Carey, *The Meeting of the Waters*, p. 161.
27 Carey, *The Meeting of the Waters*, p. 165.
28 G. K. A. Bell (ed.), *Documents on Christian Unity*, 3rd series, Oxford University Press, 1948, pp. 71–101.
29 Bell (ed.), *Documents on Christian Unity*, p. 183.
30 Bell (ed.), *Documents on Christian Unity*, p. 185.
31 C. O. Buchanan *et al.*, *Growing into Union*, SPCK, 1970, pp. 132–3.
32 John Wenham, *The Renewal and Unity of the Church in England*, SPCK, 1972, pp. 65–6.
33 Tinker, 'Towards an Evangelical View of the Church', p. 109.
34 *May They All Be One, A Response of the House of Bishops of the Church of England to Ut Unum Sint*, House of Bishops Occasional Paper, Church House Publishing, 1997, p. 17.
35 *May They All Be One*, p. 17.
36 *May They All Be One*, p. 18.
37 R. Bewes, 'Evangelical Reaction: ARCIC is offensive', *Church of England Newspaper*, 2 July 1999, p. 12.

Chapter 4

1 I.e. those 39 books of the Old Testament and 27 books of the New Testament which Article VI of the Thirty-Nine Articles describes as follows: 'In the name of the Holy Scripture we do understand those Canonical Books of the Old and New Testament, of whose authority was never any doubt in the Church.'
2 Anglican–Roman Catholic International Commission (ARCIC), *The Final Report*, CTS/SPCK, 1982.
3 ARCIC I, *The Final Report*, Authority I, Elucidation 2.
4 ARCIC I, *The Final Report*, Authority I, Elucidation 2.
5 *Towards a Church of England Response to BEM and ARCIC*, CIO Publishing, 1985, paragraph 214.
6 Second Anglican–Roman Catholic International Commission, *The Gift of Authority: Authority in the Church III*, CTS/Church Publishing Incorporated, 1999.
7 *The Gift of Authority*, Preface.
8 *The Gift of Authority*, The Status of the Document.
9 *The Gift of Authority*, paragraph 19.
10 This is true also of the Fetter Lane Common Statement (1995) of the *Anglican–Moravian Conversations*, Council for Christian

Unity of the General Synod, 1996. See paragraph 28a in the section 'What we can now agree in faith'.

11 See Appendix for an analysis of biblical references in some of the main dialogues. It is interesting to note that, particularly in Anglican–Protestant dialogues, relatively few references are included in sections on ministry.

12 Pullach Report, *Anglican–Lutheran International Conversations 1970–1972*, SPCK, 1973, paragraphs 20, 21; cf. *God's Reign and Our Unity*, SPCK/St Andrew Press, 1984, paragraph 40.

13 Pullach Report, paragraph 22.

14 ARCIC I, *The Final Report, Authority I, Elucidation 2*; cf. *God's Reign and Our Unity*, paragraph 40.

15 ARCIC I, *The Final Report, Authority I, Elucidation 2*.

16 *The Gift of Authority*, paragraph 20.

17 *The Gift of Authority*, paragraphs 24, 25.

18 *The Gift of Authority*, paragraph 24.

19 *The Gift of Authority*, paragraph 23.

20 See, e.g., *The Gift of Authority*, paragraph 20.

21 *'Trustworthy and True', Pastoral Letters from the Lambeth Conference 1988*, Church House Publishing, 1988, pp. 1–2.

22 The report of the Commission is included in the published proceedings of the Lambeth Conference 1998: *The Virginia Report, The Report of the Inter-Anglican Theological and Doctrinal Commission*, Morehouse Publishing, 1999.

23 *The Virginia Report*, p. 32.

24 *The Virginia Report*, p. 32.

25 *The Virginia Report*, p. 33.

26 *The Virginia Report*, p. 33.

Chapter 5

1 *Baptism, Eucharist and Ministry*, Faith and Order Paper 111, WCC, 1982.

2 *Baptism, Eucharist and Ministry 1982–1990: Report on the Process and the Responses*, Faith and Order Paper 149, WCC Publications, 1990, p. vii.

3 *Baptism, Eucharist and Ministry*, p. ix.

4 H. N. Bate (ed.), *Proceedings of the World Conference, Lausanne, August 3–21, 1927*, Doubleday, Doran, 1928, p. 476.

5 L. Vischer (ed.), *A Documentary History of the Faith and Order Movement 1927–1963*, Bethany Press, 1963, pp. 44, 100.

6 G. Gassmann (ed.), *Documentary History of Faith and Order, 1963–1993*, WCC Publications, 1993, §45, p. 11.

7   *Baptism, Eucharist and Ministry*, p. ix.
8   A helpful survey of the development of interest in hermeneutics within ecumenical circles can be found in A. Houtepen, 'Hermeneutics and Ecumenism: The Art of Understanding a Communicative God', in P. Bouteneff and D. Heller (eds), *Interpreting Together: Essays in Hermeneutics*, WCC Publications, 2001, pp. 1–18, pp. 7–15.
9   P. Bouteneff and D. Heller, 'Preface', in P. Bouteneff and D. Heller (eds), *Interpreting Together: Essays in Hermeneutics*, WCC Publications, 2001, p. ix.
10 *A Treasure in Earthen Vessels: An Instrument for an Ecumenical Reflection on Hermeneutics*, Faith and Order Paper 182, WCC Publications, 1998.
11 Bouteneff and Heller, *Interpreting Together*.
12 M. Thurian, 'Introduction', in M. Thurian (ed.), *Churches Respond to BEM: Official responses to the 'Baptism, Eucharist and Ministry' text*, Faith and Order Paper 129, WCC, 1986, p. 4.
13 *Baptism, Eucharist and Ministry*, p. 2.
14 *Baptism, Eucharist and Ministry*, p. 20.
15 W. Tabbernee, 'BEM and the Eucharist: A Case Study in Ecumenical Hermeneutics', in P. Bouteneff and D. Heller (eds), *Interpreting Together: Essays in Hermeneutics*, WCC Publications, 2001, pp. 19–46, pp. 26–37.
16 Gassmann (ed.), *Documentary History of Faith and Order*, §45, p. 11.
17 *Baptism, Eucharist and Ministry*, p. 3.
18 See, for example, Pseudo-Jonathan III 'he may be established in the world to come' cited in J. Bowker, *The Targums and Rabbinic Literature: An Introduction to Jewish Interpretations of Scripture*, Cambridge University Press, 1969, p. 124.
19 Gassmann (ed.), *Documentary History of Faith and Order*, §45, p. 11.
20 *Baptism, Eucharist and Ministry*, p. 21.
21 Thurian, *Churches Respond to BEM*, p. 4.
22 Tabbernee, 'BEM and the Eucharist', p. 19.
23 *Baptism, Eucharist and Ministry 1982–1990*, p. 132.
24 *Baptism, Eucharist and Ministry 1982–1990*, p. 132.
25 Tabbernee, 'BEM and the Eucharist', p. 20.
26 *Baptism, Eucharist and Ministry*, p. 2.
27 *Baptism, Eucharist and Ministry*, p. 20.
28 *Baptism, Eucharist and Ministry*, p. 10.
29 J. P. Hyatt, *Exodus*, Marshall, Morgan & Scott, 1971, pp. 253–8, although M. Noth, *Exodus: A Commentary*, SCM Press, 1962,

has argued that Exodus 24.1-14 is all by E with a few secondary additions, this has never become widely accepted in scholarship.

30   *Baptism, Eucharist and Ministry*, p. 2.
31   *Baptism, Eucharist and Ministry*, p. 2.
32   *Baptism, Eucharist and Ministry*, p. 3.
33   *Baptism, Eucharist and Ministry*, p. 4.
34   *Baptism, Eucharist and Ministry*, p. 14.
35   *Baptism, Eucharist and Ministry*, pp. 23–4.
36   H. D. Betz, *Galatians*, Hermeneia, Fortress Press, 1979, pp. 186–201; R. N. Longenecker, *Galatians*, Word Biblical Commentaries, Word, 1990, pp. 150–59.
37   Longenecker, *Galatians*, p. 151.
38   B. Witherington, 'Rite and Rights for Women – Galatians 3.28', *New Testament Studies* 27(5), 1981, pp. 593–604.
39   Witherington, 'Rite and Rights for Women'; though Longenecker, *Galatians*, p. 157, sees in this phrase simply an echo of Genesis 1.27.
40   Tabbernee, 'BEM and the Eucharist', p. 19.
41   B. Childs, *Biblical Theology in Crisis*, Fortress Press, 1970.
42   J. Barton, 'Introduction', in J. Barton (ed.), *The Cambridge Companion to Biblical Interpretation*, Cambridge University Press, 1998, p. 1.
43   Pontifical Biblical Commission, *The Interpretation of the Bible in the Church*, Libreria Editrice Vaticana, 1993.
44   Tabbernee, 'BEM and the Eucharist', p. 20.
45   *Baptism, Eucharist and Ministry*, p. 10.
46   Gassmann (ed.), *Documentary History of Faith and Order*, §45, p. 11.

Chapter 6

1   See J. D. G. Dunn, *Unity and Diversity in the New Testament*, SCM Press, 1977; J. Reumann, *Variety and Unity in New Testament Thought*, Oxford University Press, 1991.
2   G. N. Stanton, *The Gospels and Jesus*, Oxford University Press, 1989; M. Hengel, *The Four Gospels and the One Gospel of Jesus Christ*, SCM Press, 2000.
3   See A. O. Lovejoy, *The Great Chain of Being*, Harvard University Press, 1953.
4   Cf. I. Kindt-Siegwalt, 'Believing in Unity and Accepting Difference', *Ecumenical Review* 51, 1999, pp. 193–201.
5   Galatians 4.4; S. Kierkegaard, *Philosophical Fragments*, Princeton University Press, 1946, p. 13.

6   H. Meyer, *That All May be One*, Eerdmans, 1999, p. 51.
7   Cf. K. Raiser, 'That the World May Believe: The Missionary Vocation as the Necessary Horizon for Ecumenism', *International Review of Mission*, 88, 1999, p. 194.
8   ARCIC (Anglican–Roman Catholic International Commission), *The Final Report*, SPCK/CTS, 1982, p. 59, paragraph 15.
9   Cf. K. Koyama, 'A Theological Reflection on Religious Pluralism', *Ecumenical Review* 51, 1999, pp. 160–71.
10 *The Cloud of Unknowing*, trans. C. Wolters, Penguin, 1961.
11 See, for a challenging example of this approach, D. Hampson, *Christian Contradictions: The Structures of Lutheran and Catholic Thought*, Cambridge University Press, 2001.
12 Cf. K. Rahner, 'Pluralism in Theology and the Unity of the Creed in the Church', *Theological Investigations* XI, Darton, Longman & Todd/Seabury (Crossroad), 1974, pp. 3–23; S. W. Sykes, *The Identity of Christianity*, SPCK, 1984; P. Avis, *Ecumenical Theology and the Elusiveness of Doctrine*, SPCK, 1986.
13 Fetter Lane Common Statement, *Anglican–Moravian Conversations*, London, Council for Christian Unity of the General Synod, 1996, paragraph 52.
14 *Gaudium et Spes* 92, in W. M. Abbott (ed.), *The Documents of Vatican II*, Geoffrey Chapman, 1966, p. 306.
15 See J. Fameree, 'Legitimate Diversity in the Roman Catholic Tradition, with special reference to the thought of Vatican II', *One in Christ* 37.3, July 2002, pp. 25–38.
16 *God's Reign and Our Unity*, SPCK/St Andrew Press, 1984, paragraph 34.
17 Cited in G. K. A. Bell, *The Kingship of Christ*, Penguin, 1954, p. 141.
18 A. Richardson, *An Introduction to the Theology of the New Testament*, SCM Press, 1958, p. 287.

Chapter 7

1 E.g. Christoph Schwöbel, 'The Creature of the Word: Recovering the Ecclesiology of the Reformers', in C. Gunton and D. W. Hardy (eds), *On Being the Church: Essays on the Christian Community*, T&T Clark, 1989.
2 Miroslav Volf, *After Our Likeness: The Church as the Image of the Trinity*, Eerdmans, 1998.
3 Volf, *After Our Likeness*, p. 191.
4 Jürgen Moltmann, *The Trinity and the Kingdom: The Doctrine of God*, Harper & Row, 1981.

5 See Second Anglican–Roman Catholic International Commission, *Church as Communion*, Church House Publishing/ CTS, 1991.

6 *The Virginia Report: The Report of the Inter-Anglican Theological and Doctrinal Commission*, Morehouse Publishing, 1999.

7 *On the Way to Visible Unity, A Common Statement*, Meissen, 1988, paragraphs 4 & 5, The Meissen Agreement, Council for Christian Unity, 1992. This text echoes and footnotes both the earlier work of the Anglican Lutheran European Commission and the Anglican–Roman Catholic International Commission.

8 Meissen Common Statement, paragraph 3.

9 Meissen Common Statement, paragraph 5.

10 See Henry R. McAdoo, 'Unity: An Approach by Stages?', in Alan C. Clark and Colin Davey (eds), *Anglican/Roman Catholic Dialogue: The Work of the Preparatory Commission*, Oxford University Press, 1974.

11 'Recognize' has two senses in English that have sometimes led to confusion in ecumenical dialogue. I can 'recognize' a long-absent relative on meeting again. But a person or an organization can also 'recognize' another person or organization by bestowing authority or validation upon them, as when the Methodist Conference bestows the title 'recognized and regarded' on non-Methodist ministers. In German the distinction is clearer in that two words can be used: *erkennen* and *anerkennen*. To recognize unity with another Church is not to confer something by act of recognition but to acknowledge that there is something given in the other Church which unites us with it.

12 *Augsburg Confession*, VII.

13 Calvin, *Institutes* IV.i.9

14 See Oliver O'Donovan, *On the Thirty-Nine Articles: A Conversation with Tudor Christianity*, Paternoster Press, 1986, pp. 88ff.

15 See, for example, Second Anglican–Roman Catholic International Commission, *Salvation and the Church*, Church House Publishing, 1987.

16 John Wesley famously stated it was a fable no man had proved or could prove.

17 Ingolf Dalferth, 'Ministry and the Office of Bishop according to Meissen and Porvoo: Protestant Remarks about Several Unclarifed Questions', in *Visible Unity and the Ministry of Oversight: The Second Theological Conference held under the Meissen Agreement between the Church of England and the*

Evangelical Church in Germany, Church House Publishing, 1997, p. 33.

18 Dalferth, 'Ministry and the Office of Bishop', p. 19.

19 See the ARCIC Statement *Church as Communion*.

20 *God's Reign and Our Unity, The Report of the Anglican–Reformed International Commission 1981–1984*, SPCK, 1984, paragraph 29.

21 Leuenberg Church Fellowship, *The Church of Jesus Christ: The Contribution of the Reformation towards Ecumenical Dialogue on Church Unity*, Verlag Otto Lembeck, 1995, §§1 and 2.

22 *The Church of Jesus Christ*, introduction to Chapter 1.

23 See Friedrich Schleiermacher, *The Christian Faith*, 2nd edn, T&T Clark, 1960, p. 103.

24 Volf, *After Our Likeness*, p. 163.

25 See *The Church of Jesus Christ*, 2.2.

26 See W. Kasper, 'Grundkonsens und Kirchengemeinschaft: Zum Stand des ökumenischen Gesprächs zwischen katholischer und evangelisch-lutherischer Kirche', *Theologische Quartalschrift* 167, 1987, pp. 161–81 and André Birmelé, *Le salut en Jésu Christ dans les dialogues oecuméniques*, Cogitatio fidei 141, Cerf, 1986.

27 *Apostolicity and Succession*, House of Bishops Occasional Paper, General Synod of the Church of England, London, 1994, paragraph 69, D.

28 See Kasper, 'Grundkonsens', p. 176.

29 For a defence of Zizioulas, see Paul McPartlan, *The Eucharist Makes the Church: Henri de Lubac and John Zizioulas in Dialogue*, T&T Clark, 1993.

30 This homily, wrongly called the 'Homily of Justification' in Article XI, speaks of good works 'after that we are baptized or justified'.

31 Tract I, its anonymous author was John Henry Newman.

32 Ramsey grounded this emphasis in the New Testament and especially in 2 Corinthians and 1 John together with the Letters of Ignatius. See Michael Ramsey, *The Gospel and the Catholic Church*, Longmans, Green, 1936 (2nd edn 1956) pp. 48–9, 56, 78–9.

33 Ramsey, *The Gospel and the Catholic Church*, p. 201.

34 'And our view of ministry had better be evangelical than archaeological', Ramsey, *The Gospel and the Catholic Church*, p. 69.

35 Kenneth E. Kirk (ed.), *The Apostolic Ministry: Essays on the History and the Doctrine of Episcopacy*, Hodder & Stoughton, 1947.

36 Smyr. 8.2.
37 Karl Barth, *Church Dogmatics* IV/I, T&T Clark, 1956, pp. 701ff.
38 In addition to the discussion of the visibility of the Church in *Church Dogmatics* there is an interesting passage in Barth's lecture on the Apostles' Creed (commenting upon Calvin) on the relationship between the Church and the Kingdom and on 'The Faithfulness to the Visible Church': 'But the important thing is never to separate the visible Church from the invisible Church. Let us not hover over the clouds: to believe is to live. To live is to labour. To labour is to be here and not there. Concretely to live within a church.' And 'Let us clearly make this distinction: it is not a question of believing in an invisible Church, but – seeing the visible Church – of believing in the invisible Church through her earthly and present expression.' See Karl Barth, *The Faith of the Church: A commentary on the Apostles' Creed*, Fontana, 1960, p. 125.
39 This is, however, a matter of continuing debate within the Roman Catholic Church. For this debate see CDF Letter on Communion (1992); Christopher Hill, *Catholic International/One in Christ* 1992:4; Walter Kasper, *The Tablet*, June 2001.
40 See Ramsey, *The Gospel and the Catholic Church*, p. 48. With this Cardinal Ratzinger would be in agreement. It can also be construed from the language of the Declaration of Assent: 'The Church of England is part of the one holy, catholic and apostolic Church', though I do not believe this was intended.
41 André Birmelé, 'The unity of the Church: The different approaches of the Lutheran–Anglican and Lutheran–Reformed dialogues', in Colin Podmore (ed.), *Community – Unity – Communion: Essays in Honour of Mary Tanner*, Church House Publishing, 1998, p. 260.
42 Rowan Williams, 'Authority and the Bishop in the Church', in Mark Santer (ed.), *Their Lord and Ours: Approaches to Authority, Community and the Unity of the Church*, SPCK, 1982, p. 96.
43 *The Niagara Report: Report of the Anglican–Lutheran Consultation on Episcope 1987*, Church House Publishing, 1988, paragraph 7.
44 Calvin, *Institutes* IV.iii.2.
45 Calvin, *Institutes* IV.iii.2.
46 See response by John Zizioulas (Metropolitan of Pergamon) in *The Truth Shall Make You Free: The Lambeth Conference 1988. The Reports, Resolutions & Pastoral Letters from the Bishops*, Church House Publishing, 1988, pp. 283–8.

47 Geoffrey Wainwright, 'Is Episcopal Succession a Matter of Dogma for Anglicans?', in Podmore (ed.), *Community – Unity – Communion*, p. 167.

48 In the seventeenth century, Bishop Lancelot Andrewes spoke positively of the ministry of the Reformed Church of France, and Archbishop William Laud spoke of German Superintendents as differing more in sound than sense from bishops.

49 Volf, *After Our Likeness*, p. 275.

50 See Michael Root, '"Reconciled diversity" and the visible unity of the Church', in Podmore (ed.), *Community – Unity – Communion*, pp. 237–51.

51 Volf, *After Our Likeness*, p. 275.

52 Williams, 'Authority and the Bishop in the Church', p. 93.

53 Williams, 'Authority and the Bishop in the Church', p. 96.

54 Williams, 'Authority and the Bishop in the Church', p. 100.

Index of biblical references

Subject index